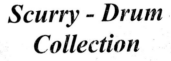

SEEKING
THE
FACE OF
GOD

*Dedicated to the memory of Dr. Klaus Bockmuehl,
a man of great faith and intellect. Although he never lived to
see it, he spoke matter-of-factly about my "writing ministry"
years before he had any earthly reason to do so. There were
plenty of students much more deserving of his attention than
I was, but Dr. Bockmuehl's gracious contribution and
encouragement have left a lasting impression. The memory of
his life continues to call me forward in Christ.*

CONTENTS

Acknowledgments

I am grateful to:

• Burt Stouffer for introducing me to Thomas Nelson Publishers and Janet Thoma

• Jerry Thomas for his helpful comments, particularly in the early stages of this project

• Doug Thorson, for the gift of his old computer that allowed me to work at home

• Those people from whom I have benefited as they invested their time and wisdom in me out of service to God, particularly my parents, E. J. and Geneva Thomas, the Rev. Eugene Boggess, Brady Bobbink, Dr. Klaus Bockmuehl, and virtually the entire staff and faculty of Regent College in Vancouver, British Columbia, in the mid-1980s, especially Dr. J. I. Packer and Dr. James Houston.

In addition, it would be difficult for me to overstate my appreciation for two people in particular. I was truly blessed to work with such a skilled and competent editor as Janet Thoma. I only wish I could write as well as she can edit. I also want to thank my wife, Lisa Thomas, who, in spite of the daily challenges of raising and home-schooling our three small children, lovingly puts up with a husband who has a full-time job and writes on the side. Without her support, this book wouldn't have been possible.

Chapter One

The Journey
of Faith

> *O Lord my God, Light of the blind, and Strength of the weak; yea also Light of those that see, and strength of the strong: hearken unto my soul, and hear it crying out of the depths.*   Augustine
>
> *"Who is he who will devote himself to be close to me?" declares the LORD.*   Jeremiah 30:21 (NIV)

When I first entered seminary, I found there was just as much ambition in my heart and the hearts of many of my classmates as you would find among those enrolled in any MBA program or law school.

That was the motivation a small group of us needed to get up at 5:00 A.M. so we could beat the tunnel traffic heading into Vancouver. We'd arrive on campus at 6:00, and since classes didn't start until 8:00 I'd usually walk over to the hospital cafeteria and spend some time alone.

The discipline of early rising turned me into a person who loved to watch the morning dawn break open. God's voice always seemed a little bit clearer then since my mind wasn't full of the day's concerns and studies. Because I went to a good school, spending time in devotion with God was stressed even above our studies, so I'd often spend these hours prayerfully meditating, studying, praying, worshiping, and listening.

It was during these hours that I believe God gave me my life's calling.

I was impressed with the fact that many had written their systematic theologies, and we needed them, but the Christian world could do very well without another one written by me. God was searching for people who would *live* the theology, incarnating the doctrines into their lives. People have written about the Christian life for years, but who would live it?

A thousand years ago, that challenge led many to give up everything, join a religious order, and focus exclusively on following Christ. A little more than a hundred years ago, that challenge led many to forsake their homelands and travel to foreign countries to focus exclusively on sharing Christ. Christians still join religious orders today, and missionaries still go overseas (and may their numbers increase), but what does it mean to live the Christian faith today in our society? What would people who took it seriously look like?

Fortunately, I was going to the right school to ask such questions. Regent College in Vancouver, British Columbia, is known for its spiritual theology. Teachers such as Dr. J. I. Packer, the late Dr. Klaus Bockmuehl, and Dr. James Houston challenged us not only to think correctly, but to love God passionately.

My thirst for God led me to begin reading the classics of the Christian faith, and I discovered new friends such as John of the Cross, John Climacus, and William Law. Over time, I began to realize some common themes, and I began to write them down. I saw that, although these saints had lived in different centuries and different countries and served God in different Christian traditions, they agreed on quite a lot; they faced some of the same struggles and arrived at many of the same answers.

They certainly weren't spouting formulas or ten easy steps. In fact, they often spoke of a spiritual desert or a dark night of the soul, and I knew they were speaking the truth. My heart sang when I realized someone else had gone through that too.

What I really want to do in this book is simply introduce you to some of these precious Christian brothers and sisters who have walked this life before us. I want to introduce you to their struggles and their insights, their victories and their defeats. Most of all, I want to help you capture not only their wisdom and practical advice, but also their passion for God.

The Cry of Our Hearts

Some might wonder how the ancients could have anything relevant to say to us today. It's true they probably couldn't comprehend the ten-thousand-member megachurches, as we know them today, or the football stadiums packed with seekers waiting to hear Billy Graham, or the satellites carrying Christian programming all over the world. But has the human heart changed also? In our race for technology, we may have lost touch with the individual human soul and the transcendent God who made us. In contrast, the precious saints I'll describe knew the ache of humanity and the glory of God like few others.

The true ache of our generation is to come into relationship with the one true and Holy God. The young man seeking to bed as many women as possible, the older man desperate to make his business a success, the young woman determined at all costs to become a doctor, the older woman sick with concern for her children—all these may not realize it, but what they really seek is to know and love God.

We can read volumes on emotional wholeness, marital and family relationships, financial responsibility, and other pressing issues (and well we should), but every book worth reading recites one familiar refrain: The foundational issue is our relationship to God. If we center our life around Him, this area will fall into place as well.

But this is like telling someone who is struggling to climb a hill, "First learn how to climb a mountain." It is no help at all, for it is saying that an even greater struggle lies before us and until that one is conquered, we are left where we are.

For how can we, encased in flesh and imprisoned in time, relate to a God who is spirit and eternal? How do we, with finite minds scarcely able to think above our sinful passions, commune with a God who is infinite in all His holy glory and in whose mind no sin has ever dwelt?

Surely there has never been a more unequal relationship than the one Christ calls us to when He says, "Come, follow Me." Our lack of wonder at the absolute inequality of the relationship is evidence enough that we do not fully comprehend the greatness of the God who speaks and the humility of us who listen.

This relationship calls us to the chief goal of humankind, "to glorify God and enjoy Him forever," as one of the great confessions says. But this itself presents a problem. What does it mean to *enjoy* God? How do we relate to One we can't see, whose voice we cannot audibly hear?

For centuries that has been the question of men and women whose hearts have burned with the holy passion of a pure and all-consuming love for their God. Through the centuries in many traditions and many lands, teenagers, adults, the elderly, and even children have heard the call of God and turned their hearts into receptacles of His grace. These saints can teach us so much. They can lift us out of our century, out of our comfortable spiritual cul-de-sacs, and out of our limited understanding and point the way to a new horizon. We may not accept every minor doctrine they teach, but we can recognize the love of God in them, and we can learn, perhaps, how that love was kindled and how they learned to enjoy God.

This book is a journal of the quest to know God—what academicians often call Christian spirituality and what one writer has described as the "life of God in the soul of man." Let's consider some specifics of what Christian spirituality is and is not before we begin to survey the wisdom of those who have preceded us on this great journey.

1. Christian Spirituality Is God-Centered, Not Man-Centered

Christian spirituality is not a search to discover ourselves or to be enlightened or even to add a new dimension to our lives. No. Christian spirituality is the search to be in relationship with God. This search is initiated by God, empowered by God, and made possible by God. Augustine wrote, "Christ carries us on, as a leader, carries us in Him, as the way, carries us up to Him, as our home."[1] God is our desire. Not power. Not experience. Not the supernatural, but God, revealed to us in Jesus Christ.

In a very real sense, then, Christian spirituality talks about what we *receive* more than what we *achieve*. Our potential and

[1] *Psalm 60*, sec. 4, cited in Augustine, *The Confessions of Saint Augustine* (New York: Airmont Publishing, 1969), 65.

activity are entirely dependent on God's prior work in our lives. If we set out to be achievers, rather than receivers, we have not begun to follow God. Achievers call attention only to themselves, whereas receivers lead others to appreciate the Giver.

If we insist on being achievers, seeking God so that others might admire our faith, our commitment, or our dedication, we become God's competitors, trying to steal some of His glory.

2. Spirituality Isn't Relative

The very word *spirituality* can sound hopelessly subjective, spooky, esoteric, mysterious. People often think of it as something "out there," unprovable, intangible, perhaps even scary. Thus an interest in this kind of spirituality is best left to those who would prefer to float above the earth, who have no more use for logic or reason than a fish has for a hat.

This is not Christian spirituality, which is anchored in biblical truth and protected by its expression in the corporate church. In some ways, spirituality can be very scientific. We might think of ourselves as pioneers, but we are so only in the sense of those pioneers who followed the deep wagon ruts of the Oregon or Santa Fe trails. Others have preceded us. Others have faced the same temptations. Others reached the same understanding. While every journey is unique, every journey also shares commonalities that have been experienced before, and every journey has the same goal—to know God. It is silly to reinvent the Christian faith generation after generation merely because we will not read the devotional writings of ancient Roman Catholics or Eastern Orthodox Christians because their theology disagrees with ours 5 or 10 percent of the time.

3. *Christian Spirituality Is Necessary to Help Others*

One of the chief aims of Christian spirituality, second only to being God-centered, is the call to be others-centered. What set Christ apart from the Pharisees is that the Pharisees sought to make themselves holy. Jesus, instead, sought to make others holy. He had an others-centered faith (within the overall context of a God-centered faith).

We glamorize evangelism and, indeed, evangelism is a holy, necessary, and primary calling. We would do well, however, to recognize "soul surgery"—the ability to take those who are suffering from spiritual problems and work with God to bring them back to spiritual health.

Every spiritual problem has an individual genesis and needs an individual exodus. Generalized preaching is crucial to the Christian community, but it is not sufficient to meet the individual needs that require individual attention. In our individual counsel to people we need to guard against simplistic answers and general platitudes that leave them impressed but still broken. Thus the need for maturity.

We do not need to be mature to reach heaven. We can experience salvation just minutes after being a practicing heathen. God answers our simple prayer for help that expresses the true cry of the heart and He immediately ushers us into the eternal kingdom. However, without maturity, we will have neither the motivation nor the ability to get involved in the lives of others.

God must do a work *in* us before He can work *through* us. That is why it is so dangerous not to grow. There is a world of human wastage out there. Some of it is due to sin; much of it is due to complacency as lives are slowly wasting away in front of television sets or in gossip sessions and any host of narcotics used by our society to escape life.

We seek a better way, the way of the cross, the way of Jesus Christ.

Beginning the Journey

If this sounds like the cry of your heart, read on, but read slowly. The wisdom of the ages cannot be grasped through sixty minutes of speed-reading. As you read, thank God for those who have gone before you, those who refused to give way in the face of temptation, those who said yes to God's cry to live as His children. Because of them, we are richer. We are their heirs, their fellow pilgrims, on the journey to a deeper walk with God.

We'll begin our journey by discussing spiritual goals. The ancients' faith was a purposeful faith, and ours must be also. The ancients also taught that we must be willing to pay the price to make our spiritual goals come true.

Next we'll turn our attention to six elements of the spiritual life that will help make possible our growth in holiness. The ancients found their spiritual growth enhanced when they built on a foundation of spiritual training, holiness, surrender, simplicity of the heart, a double-sided humility, and the constant remembrance of death.

We'll then look at two elements that tend to trip us up: difficulty and spiritual dryness. Depending upon how we face them, these two elements can divert us into a spiritual cul-de-sac or release us onto a wide avenue of growth. We'll set off on a new beginning. We'll be ready for a long-term view of the Christian journey by exploring the seasons of the soul—

how our faith changes and transforms as we mature and grow older.

And finally, we will look at our need for spiritual direction. While the ancients have much to teach us, they would also have us continue to learn through contemporary role models.

Some of these themes might seem new, but they are, of course, all very old. Every generation has a tendency to create pet sins and pet obligations. Once we step out of our generation, however, we will find a wealth of teaching not subject to our own cultural tunnel vision.

At the end of each chapter is a section entitled "Reflection." This section will use different formats but it will always have the same goal—helping you to incorporate the truth of the chapter into your life. The ancients would be very disappointed if we finished this study smarter but less holy. Together, we are not seeking concepts, but the Holy God whose truth transforms us all.

Chapter Two

Starting at the Finish Line: Spiritual Goals

> *Many there are who count how long it is since their conversion; and yet full slender oftentimes is the fruit of amendment in their lives.* Thomas à Kempis, *The Imitation of Christ*

Cheryl was a young gymnast. The competition to qualify for the national team was fierce, but Cheryl knew what she wanted to do, and she was willing to pay the price to achieve it. Her diet, her social life, her education, and her sleep all revolved around her training. At night she fell asleep thinking about the next competition. In the morning she was consumed with getting the kinks out of a particular move.

Several months later, Cheryl missed qualifying for nationals. She decided she was too old to continue and "retired" at sixteen.

Cheryl then experienced a radical transformation in her schedule, her thoughts, and her actions. It was almost as if she had a different life before and after the birth and death of her goals.

Goals move us. In business, sports, politics—and the Christian life—goals often make the difference between moving forward or going around in circles.

Starting at the Finish Line

Unfortunately, modern Christian spirituality is marked by "starting at the finish line." In this spirituality, the goal of the Christian life is salvation, but salvation is received, by definition, the instant one becomes a Christian. Because many evangelicals also believe that salvation cannot be lost, the new believer has already attained the goal of Christianity, which he or she can't lose, just seconds after being a pagan.

In other words, we've started at the finish line. All that is left to do is to hold on and wait for the awards ceremony to begin. It's like running a race with a continual backward glance, wondering if somebody is going to catch us, rather than focusing on what is ahead.

We are encouraged to grow, of course, but the motivation for growth in such a spirituality is weak. As a young campus pastor, the question I most often heard was "Can I lose my salvation?" rather than "How can I grow?" We seem to have an overwhelming desire to make it into heaven in the same way a hero barely survives at the end of a movie. We'll limp into heaven bruised and bleeding with buildings burning all around us, our clothes ripped and torn, our faces scratched, sweaty, and dirty, and our hair moving every which way in the smoke-filled air.

Most evangelicals, steeped in salvation by grace through faith, are removed from the thought of working to achieve salvation; we have rightly grasped this precious truth, but at the expense of another precious truth: the need to grow.

This has been a convenient lapse. Growth is painful. It is most frequently the result of enduring difficulty and pain. Unless we are strongly motivated to grow, the pain will be too great and we'll excuse ourselves from the obligation by saying, "Jesus already did it for me." In such a context, this is not a statement of faith; it's a statement of slothfulness. Scripture is replete with references urging us to grow.[1]

Our spiritual ancestors knew no other way. Thomas à Kempis wrote, "Our fervor and progress should increase daily: but now it is accounted a great matter, if a man can retain but some part of his first zeal."[2] He was telling us there should be a daily progress in our Christian growth. Even centuries ago, apparently, Christians were more concerned with "not falling away" than developing a mature and abiding faith.

John Climacus, one of the earliest and most popular Christian writers, went a step further when he exhorted, "Regarding every vice and every virtue, we must unceasingly scrutinize ourselves to see what point we have reached, a beginning, a middle or the end."[3] If we lack any concept of setting goals and continuing to grow, we'll have no idea whether we are stuck at the beginning, complacent at the middle, or making progress toward the end.

Thomas à Kempis and John Climacus are just two examples of Christian saints who urged the church of their day to shun complacency. Historical Christianity reserves spiritual retirement for heaven. In many cases, the uncertainty of entering heaven provoked Christians to train and guard their hearts and minds to an almost neurotic degree. We don't want to go

[1]The biblical exhortations to grow are too numerous to fully discuss here, but see 2 Peter 3:18; Colossians 1:10–12; 2 Thessalonians 1:3; and Philippians 2:12–13 for a sampling.

[2]Thomas à Kempis, *The Imitation of Christ*, ed. Paul Bechtel (Chicago: Moody Press, 1980), 1:11:5.

[3]John Climacus, *The Ladder of Divine Ascent*, trans. by Colm Luibheid and Norman Russell (New York: Paulist Press, 1984), 239.

back to that, but we can learn from the urgency of their faith. As we explore the classics of Christian literature and spirituality, we will see that those who had a particularly vibrant walk with God first had a clear picture of what they wanted to become.

A Clear Goal

Our first step in rediscovering an authentic Christian spirituality is to gain a clear picture of a mature Christian. If we ignore this question, spiritual growth will become an accidental occurrence. God has His way of making us grow regardless of circumstances, but when He is forced to move without our cooperation, growth becomes haphazard and slower than it need be.

It will be helpful to discuss many of the goals that Christians have adopted through the ages. Some of these goals may not fit within a traditional evangelical framework, but by becoming familiar with them you may find it easier to develop some spiritual goals of your own.

Climacus sought to draw believers to what he called "dispassion." This is not a passion*less* existence but a redirecting of worldly passions into heavenly longings. "Many have been speedily forgiven their sins," he said. "But no one has rapidly acquired dispassion, for this requires much time and longing, and God."[4]

John of the Cross, a monk who lived in the sixteenth century, spoke often of "divine union," a sort of spiritual marriage one experiences only after traveling through the "dark night

[4]Climacus, *The Ladder of Divine Ascent*, 259.

of the soul," a particularly difficult stage of the spiritual journey. The "divine union" calls for the renunciation of everything else so one may be completely and utterly devoted to God. The union is not achieved in a day or even in a decade, wrote John. It requires a lifetime of service and dedication, and even then its achievement is not guaranteed.

The anonymous writer of *The Cloud of Unknowing* wrote of beholding "the naked being of God." Standing in the way, however, is a darkness that must be overcome. This writer urged Christians to "step above [the darkness] with great courage and determination, and with a devout and pleasant stirring of love, and [try] to pierce that darkness which is above you. You are to strike that thick cloud of unknowing with a sharp dart of longing love; and you are not to retreat no matter what comes to pass."[5]

The primary difficulty of these goals for me is that all of them assume one is living in a religious community. They still challenge me, however, for if these people, who devoted virtually every waking moment to seeking intimacy with God, still found it necessary to establish clear goals, how much more do I—having to face the daily distractions of a job, a family, and modern society—need to keep a clear goal in focus if I'm to stay on the narrow way.

The benefit of having a goal became especially clear to me when I encountered Teresa of Avila, a famous woman of prayer who was a contemporary and acquaintance of John of the Cross in the sixteenth century. In high school and college (before I had a job, a mortgage, and kids), I used to think the only measure of a maturing prayer life was increasing the

[5]Anonymous, *The Cloud of Unknowing*, trans. Ira Progoff (New York: Dell Publishing Co., 1983), VI:4.

amount of time I spent in prayer. Thus I reasoned if I regularly prayed thirty minutes a day, to grow I'd have to pray forty-five minutes a day, and then sixty minutes a day, and then throw in some all-night vigils and on and on.

That's why I found Teresa's writings so intriguing. She carefully guided readers through six stages of prayer until they finally reached the seventh stage, the ultimate goal, which she called the "interior castle." Her writings establish a mature standard of prayer. Teresa's goal moved me to exchange my "punch-card" prayer goals for increasing *intimacy*, something that can't be measured by a clock.

These writers—John Climacus, John of the Cross, and Teresa of Avila—had one thing in common: a clear goal that shaped their Christian lives. Each goal was different, but each individual could taste, see, and smell it. In this they are not unlike the modern athletes driven to complete another workout as they dream of one day winning a gold medal. They never lose sight of the prize.

Notice that all these goals can be obtained and are sought within our earthly bodies, prior to our being taken up to heaven. In the opinion of the classics, heaven's final goal needn't preclude having earthly goals. It's clear that we are, in fact, acting somewhat without precedent when we imply that heaven is our only goal.

Where does this leave us today? Suggesting sanctification (holiness) as a goal is helpful only insofar as people understand what sanctification is and why it is necessary. It has been my experience that many Christians have only the most general notion of what true sanctification entails. This often creates soft Christians who are unwilling to face the pain that comes with growth. And who can blame them? We know we don't have to fast to be saved, so why endure the hunger pangs?

Why struggle in earthly prayer when it will come so easily in heaven? We may even be tempted to think (and this is where it gets truly perilous) that since we already have salvation and we know we'll be forgiven, why not taste the sweets of a minor sin—just a taste, not a meal—and then quickly repent before we die?

On the other hand, many want to grow, and their thirst for God only increases as time goes by. We do not serve them by failing to answer their questions: "Can I measure my advancement?" "Is it based on the things I don't do balanced with the good things I do? That doesn't sound right, but then how do I know if I'm growing?"

One of the primary needs of the evangelical church today is a clear goal that Christians can look forward to as they seek to grow. This goal will have to fit within our theological framework of salvation being hidden in God. (Not all evangelicals necessarily adhere to "eternal security," but many do.) A goal widely adopted by the church today would need to be able to encourage people to think past salvation to a deeper, more meaningful walk with God. Some people who are touching the goal should be able to explain it, describe what they did to get there, and explain how others can follow along.

I am not convinced that there should be one goal for all Christians. The activist will naturally choose a different goal than the intellectual, and the contemplative will choose yet a third; but every Christian will benefit by having some goal.

The Gospel of Mark challenged me to seek a particular goal; I share it here not necessarily as a goal for every Christian to follow, but as an example of what I'm talking about and to demonstrate the questions I asked as I sought to follow the ancients' advice on setting a spiritual goal. Jesus became my model.

Jesus as the Model

As I sought to develop a goal, I wanted to particularly avoid falling into the exclusive, "just God and me" mentality. Remember the discussion in the last chapter about how an authentic spirituality leads us to be others-centered? When our questions are simply, "How can I become holy, how can I grow, how can I reach an advanced spiritual state?" we may be doing nothing more than giving approval to an unhealthy, selfish preoccupation. Spiritual advancement is a good aim, but on its own it seems radically unlike the primary focus of Jesus, who told the story of the good Samaritan, who said we should love our neighbor and make disciples of all nations.

This, of course, immediately casts us back into a centuries-old argument about the "way of action" versus the "way of contemplation." As Christians set spiritual goals, inner growth (including prayer and the way of contemplation) was often seen as superior to serving others, the way of social action. Thus grew the concept of forsaking the world to go into the desert or establish a monastery.

If we take Jesus as our model, we see that having to choose one or the other creates a false dichotomy. Jesus was active, though not prematurely so. He waited until He was thirty to begin His public ministry. And when He became active, He never lost His spiritual center. He regularly retreated into solitude and prayer.

Jesus' life, then, provided the first clue for my goal—contemplation (prayer, meditation, time alone with God) balanced with public ministry (teaching, healing, ministering to the poor). The two are not set against each other but joined together in a cooperative effort.

Christ's teaching provided the second clue. In that teaching we see an insistence that defines the love of God as including loving and serving others. When Jesus was asked about the greatest commandment, He answered by giving *two* commandments—loving God *and our neighbor* (Matt. 22:36–40)—as if to say it is improper to describe the entire life of the Christian as an exclusive one-on-one relationship with the Father.

When Jesus wanted Peter to renew his love for Him, He required two statements—a profession of love for Jesus and a willingness to "tend My sheep" (John 21:16 NKJV).

The only goal I was to adopt, then, had to direct me to be others-centered after it led me to be God-centered. It would have to take into account Christ's pattern of prayer but also include His ministry that followed prayer. The Gospel of Mark pointed me to such a goal.

Hell Breaking Apart at Jesus' Feet

When I was reading the first chapter of Mark in search of my goal, it was almost as if I was transported into the first century and could experience the awe, the fear, and the excitement many people must have felt as they saw Jesus in action. The people of the first century were trapped in their physical illnesses, spiritual prisons, and physical deprivations. Yet here walked a liberated man, subject, it seemed, to none of these prisons—One who even carried the keys to release others from them.

The awe the people felt when they saw Jesus move was not due to a ring of light around His head or a spotlessly clean white robe upon His back; it was because His presence and His power gave them hope that perhaps a new day and a new existence lay ahead. Three elements marked Christ's ministry—teaching, defeating the demonic, and releasing the oppressed (or healing the sick)—and all of them are described in the first chapter of Mark.

Mark wrote that as Jesus began to preach, the people were "amazed," "struck with panic," or "overwhelmed with astonishment," depending on how you choose to translate the Greek (v. 22).[6] All options point to Jesus' teaching as having a power and authority that was hitherto unknown.

Jesus' teaching did more than stir up the crowds, however. It also stirred up the demons. The two verses (23–24) following the description of Christ's teaching mention that a possessed man cried out and was then exorcised. Jesus didn't necessarily schedule an exorcism. The confrontation just happened as Christ performed His ministry.

As soon as Jesus left the site of the teaching and the exorcism, He went to Peter's home and healed Peter's mother-in-law. Again, this wasn't part of a carefully planned schedule. Jesus didn't have to script His day. His ministry was the natural outpouring of a tremendous individual walking step-by-step with the Father.

Jesus chased out ignorance, defeated the demonic, and released the ill and oppressed. In other words, as Jesus walked, *hell broke apart at His feet.*

Jesus and hell could *not* occupy the same spot, so wherever Jesus went, hell was dismantled. Together, Jesus' life and teaching provide a clear goal—seeing hell break apart at our feet and the coming forth of the kingdom of God.

During seminary I worked part-time at a public utility to pay some of my bills. One night as I was praying, the Lord kept bringing a specific woman to mind. The next morning, I was making some copies in the copyroom when this same woman walked in. I asked her how she was doing. She re-

[6]The Greek word is *exeplessonto*. The options chosen are taken from Zerwick and Grosvenor's *A Grammatical Analysis of the Greek New Testament* (Rome: Biblical Institute Press, 1981), 102.

sponded with a quick "fine," but I felt impressed to ask a more direct question, so I mentioned her husband. Immediately, the woman broke into tears.

She and her husband were both Christians but were going through a very difficult time in their marriage; she didn't know if they would make it and she just wanted her husband to make up his mind: Yes or no—was he going to stay?

It was early in the day, before many people had arrived, so we had about fifteen minutes to talk. I knew this woman needed far more than I could give her, but I also knew God had called me the night before to function as a stopgap measure. We talked and prayed, and the woman left—not completely healed, of course, but having been able to vent her frustration and gain a new perspective. The conversation didn't change her life but it did change her day, and one day matters to God just as one person matters to Him.

Another time I felt God calling me to write to the editor of a Christian publication and encourage her. I did so, then forgot about the letter until I received a reply. The editor told me she had been recently widowed. She and her husband had run the publication together for several years, but the issue I wrote about was the first one she had done by herself since her husband had died. After she had sent it out, she was plagued with doubts and confusion: Could she go on without her husband? Should she keep writing or let the publication die with her spouse?

As she read my letter, she knew God had heard her cries, and though she cried again, the tears were expressions of joy and relief, not sorrow and pain.

Satan is everywhere, discouraging and accusing Christians, especially after they step out into ministry. God wants to encourage and build up the body, and He'll often use us to do it—if we're available.

I've had other experiences where I'm simply talking with friends or acquaintances and problems will come to mind. Sometimes these problems are hidden attitudes or sins, slowly eating away at a person's spiritual life or marriage. Someone may be believing a lie or living a lie, and in the presence of God lies are exposed.

We needn't be overly concerned with the miraculous. If it happens, it happens. What is usually of even greater testimony is the ability to meet people one-on-one where they are and cooperate as God leads them out of their own private hell.

When our goals reach beyond making it into heaven to a life of ministry and impact here on earth, maturity does matter. I can be immature and reach heaven. I'm not sure, however, that I can remain immature and see hell break apart at my feet. If I am steeped in habitual sin, if I remain a spiritual adolescent, I cannot threaten hell, not while kissing its feet or lusting after its trinkets.

The goal I adopted—seeing hell break apart at my feet— encourages me to grow, not just for my own sake, but for the sake of others. It urges me to walk more closely with God so that I can be His coworker and carry on the work of Christ as I commune with Him.

We can't fake this kind of maturity. We can't impress Satan with a mask. In fact, we are liable to be run over if we pretend.[7]

If we don't experience the dissolution of hell in our own lives, we would do well to ask ourselves why. Are we flirting

[7]Witness the account in Acts 19:13–16.

with hell and thus unable to confront it? Have we refused to deal with needy issues in our lives, perhaps denying they exist, and therefore blinded ourselves to the needs and hurts of others? Or have we just become lazy, content to coast into heaven rather than be faithful servants?

This goal, to love God so much that we overflow with love for others and consequently see hell break apart at our feet, encourages us to press on to be the type of person God can use consistently and powerfully. It spurs us on toward active ministry surrounded by times of intimate prayer—for we dare not enter this ministry without the sure presence of God. The goal is also clearly defined by a central question: Are people around us being changed?

I found that my goal had been adopted by other Christians as well. They may have used slightly different terms in their time, but the substance was the same. H. A. Walters is one writer from the earlier part of this century whose words about changing others confirmed the direction of my goal. "We of Christ's army need to remember our great task of the conservation of personality for the highest ends, as we seek to prevent the fearful human wastage taking place all about us through the ravages of sin. This task is not just the comparatively simple one of passing on a word of testimony that 'Jesus Saves.' We are the human engineers by whom what is wrong with these intricate spiritual machines around us should be corrected."[8]

Walters argued that the terms *Christian* and *life-changer* ought to be interchangeable. The reason they are not, he said, includes spiritual laziness, cowardice, or sin that has paralyzed our energies. All of the blocks "point back to the

[8]H. A. Walters, *Soul Surgery* (London: Blandford Press, 1919), 19–20.

lack of vital experience of the living Christ, out of which must flow the zeal, courage, tact, and consistent Christian living which make personal work possible and fruitful."[9]

Walters also tied intimacy with God with effective personal ministry that sees people change. If our goal is a good one, others will have thought about it first.

Setting Your Own Goals

Some of you may think the goal I have adopted doesn't fit your life right now, or perhaps you believe you need something smaller or more concrete. That's fine. I have "minigoals" within the context of this larger goal. At one point my goal focused on prayer; at another, I was determined to become wiser. More recently I've been trying to focus on cultivating gentleness.

For those of you who want to explore this idea further, I'll mention some of the steps I found helpful as I sought to follow the ancients' example of establishing clear spiritual goals.

1. Review the Gospels. Spend some time rereading the Gospels and compare yourself with Christ. Does His courage confront your fear? Does His compassion for sinners call your accusing spirit into question? If you answered yes to either question, you immediately have a possible goal—to become courageous or compassionate like Christ.

2. Familiarize yourself with historical goals. Reread the goals of John Climacus, John of the Cross, Teresa of Avila, or research the goals of others. Get a feel for what the ancients were aiming at. As your reading becomes broader you'll be able to formulate goals that are less culturally conditioned and

[9]Ibid., 18.

more in line with what God really wants to do in your life. You'll also be able to confirm your goals; the writings of H. A. Walters refined my thoughts and helped to shape my conclusions.

3. Prayerfully review your goal. Spend some time in prayer and talk over your goal with God. Have you chosen one He's placed on you—is this what God wants to do at this time in your life? Let your goal be redirected and recrafted or affirmed.

4. Tell some significant others. Find a small group of people to whom you can explain your goal. Ask them to pray for you, and seek their counsel about how you can let the Spirit amend your life. Be open to their correction; you may think you need to step out in a particular area of ministry and they may say you need to put in order a few things in your own life first. Because of sin's power to deceive, goals should ideally be set and discussed in community, not isolation.

5. Get more input. Use a Bible concordance to look up relevant verses once you're relatively certain of your goal. If you know of a good book that addresses your goal, buy it and *read it twice.* Spend some time on this one area rather than trying to improve everything at once.

6. Remember where you're going. The important thing is to have a sense of how you need to grow. Figure out some way to measure it (spiritual journals can be very helpful in this regard). If you set a goal and then forget it, you're no better off than those who have never set one.

Reflections

Read Numbers 14:20–38. The people of Israel spent forty years wandering in the desert because they were afraid to grasp the goal God had given them—the promised land. Have you been wandering aimlessly like Israel, taking forty years for a journey that could be completed in three days?

Prayerfully read the first chapter of Mark. Imagine watching Jesus teach, confront the demonic, and heal Peter's mother-in-law. See how hell breaks apart at His feet.

Is hell breaking apart at your feet? Why not? Are you enamored by a small corner of hell? Are you ignoring the intimacy with God that results in a powerful ministry? The rest of this book will provide models and paradigms aimed at increasing your spiritual growth. Before you can establish a fuller program for spiritual growth, however, you might have to live with a temporary awareness of your need.

Chapter Three

Training the Body and Soul: Seven Methods of Spiritual Training

---

According to our purpose shall be the success of our spiritual progress; and much diligence is necessary to him that will show progress. And if he that firmly purposeth often faileth, what shall he do that seldom purposeth anything, or with little resolution?　　Thomas à Kempis

Train yourself to be godly.　　1 Timothy 4:7 (NIV)

When I was growing up I was an avid tennis player, practically living at a local tennis club during the summer. One of the popular books at that time was called *Inner Tennis*. I don't remember much about the book except that it stressed imagining the successful completion of what you were about to do—serving that ace, hitting that crosscourt backhand passing shot, mutilating your opponent at the net . . .

The only problem was, thinking all day couldn't make my backhand behave if I ignored drilling with the ball machine. You can meditate on tennis all day long, but who is going to improve more—the one who hits backhands for several hours or the one who sits and thinks?

It's a tempting notion, though—that if I could just think myself rich, athletic, or holy, then I would be. It's not surprising that many versions of "inner spirituality" have come awfully close to imitating the message of *Inner Tennis* because the thought is so inviting. "Think and be, think and be, think and be . . ."

While this contains an element of truth (the mind is a very powerful tool for good or evil), it ignores the fact that in addition to sinful souls and minds, we also have often-unwilling bodies. Our minds are very powerful elements of our persons, but they're not the only elements. If we don't address our bodies, holiness will feel like a cheap, ill-fitting pair of shoes that pinch our feet when we walk. We can get lost in reverie all we want, but every time we take a step, our toes will scream their defiance.

Thus it should be no surprise that the spiritual classics spend a good deal of time talking about training in the spiritual life. It's not enough to set challenging goals (the work of our minds)—we have to be willing to pay the price to make them come true.

Sick Souls Need Purposeful Spirituality

We might ask ourselves, "Why must I labor? Why is training even necessary?" The answer is that we live as very fallen people in a very fallen world. We don't realize how sick we are. Blaise Pascal's words bring us back to reality: "The figure used in the Gospel for the state of the soul that is sick is that of sick bodies. But, because one body cannot be sick enough to express it properly, there had to be more than one. Thus we find the deaf man, the dumb man, the blind man, the paralytic, dead Lazarus, the man possessed of a devil. All these put together are in the sick soul."[1]

Overcoming years of slothfulness, selfish ambition, greed, pride, and other attitudes and sins requires a life of training. If we let down our guard for just a second, sin is right there to claim us.[2] John Climacus warned, "We cannot afford to slip into carelessness even for an instant at any time up to the moment of death."[3]

We train not just because we have sick souls, however, but because spiritual growth doesn't happen by accident. Certainly God is the active agent, teaching us and moving us forward in spite of our weaknesses and failures. But the majority of our spiritual forebears agreed that God's grace shouldn't preclude our cooperation.

Two spiritual writers in particular saw the need for focused training in the spiritual life. Thomas à Kempis's classic work, *The Imitation of Christ,* emphasizes a purposeful Christianity that strives for continued growth. He wrote, "Who hath a greater combat than he that laboreth to overcome himself? This ought to be our endeavor, to conquer ourselves, and daily to wax stronger and to make a further growth in holiness."[4]

According to à Kempis, there is little progress without purpose. "According to our purpose shall be the success of our spiritual progress; and much diligence is necessary to him

[1]Blaise Pascal, *Pensées*, trans. A. J. Krailsheimer (London: the Penguin Group, 1966), 323.

[2]"My son, thou art never secure in this life, but as long as thou livest, thou shalt always need spiritual armor. Thou dwellest among enemies, and art assaulted on the right hand and on the left. If therefore thou defend not thyself on every side with the shield of patience, thou wilt not be long without a wound" (à Kempis, *The Imitation of Christ*, III:35:1).

[3]Climacus, *The Ladder of Divine Ascent*, 258.

[4]à Kempis, *The Imitation of Christ*, I:3:3.

that will show progress. And if he that firmly purposeth often faileth, what shall he do that seldom purposeth anything, or with little resolution?"[5]

In the last chapter we discussed the importance of goals; in this chapter we'll see that goals aren't achieved without a purposeful commitment. If we look at our lives and can't see any measurable spiritual growth over the past several years, we might ask ourselves, "Have I applied myself to growth? Have I cooperated with God's sanctifying work in my life? Or have I relied on spiritual osmosis—hanging around spiritual people in hopes some of it will rub off?"

Please don't fall into the trap of picturing a goal and then assuming the goal is achieved. Pascal warned, "Men often take their imagination for their heart, and often believe they are converted as soon as they start thinking of becoming converted."[6] One of Satan's favorite traps is to let us acknowledge God's conviction, then cause us to mistakenly assume that just because we are convicted we are changed.

A number of years ago a wise campus pastor, Brady Bobbink, challenged me on this issue. We were talking over one of my failures, and I casually mentioned that I saw my fault and the same situation wouldn't happen again.

"How do you know?" Brady asked me. "What are you going to do to ensure it won't?"

I learned from that encounter that sin's power needs more than an "I'm sorry" to be defeated. It often needs a plan.

I know this sounds awful. It sounds like a lot of work, but growth takes work. Salvation is free, but maturity comes with a price.

[5]Ibid., I:19:2.
[6]Pascal, *Pensées*, 347.

Thomas à Kempis's book inspired William Law to take the notion of purposeful spirituality one step further in his work entitled *A Serious Call to a Devout and Holy Life*. Law wrote, "Many will fail of their salvation, not because they took no pains or care about it, but because they did not take pains and care enough; they only sought, but did not strive to enter in."[7]

These would be the Christians who set goals and gave it a good try—for a month or so. They quickly grew tired, however, and the goal was dismissed as a "good idea in principle, but it just wasn't realistic." Setting goals but being unwilling to train toward them leaves us worse off than ignoring goals altogether, for we have done nothing but add an element of insincerity to our lives.

William Law lived and wrote in a generation of insincerity. He saw what laissez faire spirituality was doing to his countrymen. In eighteenth-century England, the era of the Enlightenment, faith was questioned and compromised lifestyles were the norm. The church was a profession for gentlemen and required nothing but a proper education. Unusual aspirations to devotion or holiness were considered "un-English" and fanatical, even for clergymen. Christianity was reduced to something respectable people believed in.[8]

To this generation, William Law wrote his non-compromising treatise, *A Serious Call to a Devout and Holy Life*. Religion, William Law argued, is not the "spice" of the proper English life; it is the *essence* of a Christian's existence. Respectability

[7]William Law, *A Serious Call to a Devout and Holy Life* (New York: Paulist Press, 1978), 66.

[8]Based on observations made by Austin Warren in "William Law: Ascetic and Mystic," in *William Law: A Serious Call to a Devout and Holy Life/The Spirit of Love, The Classics of Western Spirituality* (New York: Paulist Press, 1978), 11.

and reformed manners are not enough. Our faith in Christ should be our primary concern, and that means we must invest the time and energy necessary to become better Christians.

"It is amazing to see how eagerly men employ their parts, their sagacity, time, study, application, and exercise, how all helps are called to their assistance when anything is intended and desired in worldly matters, and how dull, negligent, and unimproved they are, how little they use their parts, sagacity, and abilities to raise and increase their devotion!"[9]

We know we can't succeed in school, business, marriage, parenting, sports, or most other endeavors without purposefully applying ourselves to moving forward; yet so many of us fail to realize the same is true of spiritual growth. Law went on to say, "The spirit of devotion [is] like any other sense or understanding that is only to be improved by study, care, application, and the use of such means and helps as are necessary to make a man proficient in any art or science."[10]

As part of this purposeful spirituality, Law urges his readers, "You are to nourish your spirits with pious readings and holy meditations, with watchings, fastings, and prayers, that you may taste and relish and desire that eternal state which is to begin when this life ends."[11]

This type of spirituality requires more than five minutes' thought every day. It requires more than a one-hour-per-week, Sunday morning tune-up. What both Law and à Kempis teach us is that our bodies and souls need training and our spirits need nourishment. Law warned his readers, "Unless

[9]Law, *A Serious Call*, 204.
[10]Ibid., 205.
[11]Ibid., 270.

holy fears animate our endeavors and keep our consciences strict and tender about every part of our duty, constantly examining how we live and how fit we are to die, we shall in all probability fall into a state of negligence and sit down in such a course of life as will never carry us to the rewards of Heaven."[12]

Foundational to spiritual training are the spiritual disciplines—Law mentions "fastings and prayers" as two such elements. So much very good material has been written in the past decade or two concerning the traditional spiritual disciplines that we don't need to repeat their teaching here. Other aspects of Christian training, however, have been lost or de-emphasized. Let's look at seven of the forgotten or neglected methods of spiritual training.

1. Pious Readings

If we want to start a successful business, we should talk to successful businesspeople. If we want advice on raising our kids, we should find a parent whose family we admire. If we want to grow in the Christian faith, who better to turn to than those who write about it from the vantage point of maturity?

Thomas à Kempis was committed to the truth of Scripture, but he also found great benefit in reading the wisdom passed down from those he called "the holy fathers." Listen to his almost reverent appreciation: "How great zeal and care had they of their spiritual progress! How strong a combat had they for the overcoming of their lusts! How pure and upright intentions kept they toward God. In the day they labored and in the night they attended to continual prayer: although when

[12]Ibid., 67.

they labored, also, they ceased not from mental prayer. They spent all their time with profit; every hour seemed short for the service of God."[13]

William Law joined Thomas à Kempis in his appreciation for "pious readings" of the Christian classics. Law chastised his fellow Englishmen for taking great pains to read the antiquities, the classics of Greek literature, and neglecting the Christian antiquities that would train them in matters of the soul. He wrote:

> Why then must the Bible lie alone in your study? Is not the spirit of the Saints, the piety of the holy followers of Jesus Christ, as good and necessary a means of entering into the spirit and taste of the gospel as the reading of the ancients is of entering into the spirit of antiquity?
>
> Is the spirit of poetry only to be got by much reading of poets and orators? And is not the spirit of devotion to be got in the same way, by frequent reading the holy thoughts and pious strains of devout men? . . . Is it not . . . reasonable for him who desires to improve in the divine life, that is, in the heavenly things, to search after every strain of devotion that may move, kindle, and inflame the holy ardor of his soul?[14]

The practice of pious readings served William Law well. He was able to rise above the limitations of his "respectable" culture to find a way to true and sincere faith by feeding at the table of Thomas à Kempis and others who sought the same God in a different century, and that's what I think is so important about reading the classics. It removes our generational blinders. Law could critique his fellow countrymen and

[13]à Kempis, *The Imitation of Christ*, I:18:2-3.
[14]Law, *A Serious Call*, 206-7.

arm himself against the prejudices of his day by reading outside his generation.

This past year at a conference in Virginia I taught a workshop entitled "Building a Spiritual Foundation for Ministry." Several of the evaluations contained remarks such as, "Thanks for not simply reinventing the wheel." I smiled because everything I taught was purposefully lifted from the Christian classics, and I acknowledged that at the conference. I *did* reinvent the wheel—it just wasn't a twentieth-century wheel, so it seemed new to twentieth-century Christians.

The practice of pious readings not only inflames us with John of the Cross's passion for God, John Climacus's willingness to suffer for God, and William Law's commitment to progress in God, but it also chips away at our personal prejudices. I rarely hear a sermon (in fact, I don't remember hearing one) that talks about pride with the same seriousness that you read about it in the classics. Our evangelical culture seems preoccupied with sexual sin and greed, but the ancients usually talked about pride and the need to love others.

I don't think it's a coincidence that Christians today are seen as very self-righteous and proud. In some of our statements and preaching we do seem full of ourselves. We have an answer, book, or sermon for every problem imaginable, and in our zeal to share the good news we forget that repentance is the house of the Christian life, not just the doorway. (We'll talk more about the ancients' view of humility and pride in a later chapter, but this is just one example of how I have been particularly challenged by the "lost" wisdom of saints who walked the same journey hundreds or even more than a thousand years ago.)

A number of years ago, Dr. James Houston, a professor of spirituality at Regent College, encouraged us seminarians to read Teresa of Avila. Why? Because she was as different from most of us as anyone could possibly be. She was from another country, another century, and another tradition. She was female, and most of us were male. She wrote *The Interior Castle* near the end of her life, and most of us were at the beginning of ours. She could provide answers to questions we didn't even know to ask.

I found Teresa's commitment to prayerful intimacy with God very challenging. Prayer was often a battle cry for me— "Here I go, Lord; please come with me!"—until Teresa urged me to settle down and seek an intimacy far removed from works. It was natural for Teresa, a woman, to seek to become the bride of Christ, but how could I, a male, have the same intimacy?

Teresa couldn't fully answer this question for me, though she pointed me in the right direction; but I found some additional assistance in the works of Andrew Murray, a rather modern writer if judged by the standards of the classics. Soon my prayer wasn't just "Thy kingdom come—today!" but "My precious Lord, I want to be often and long alone with You."

I realized how much I had changed when an Episcopalian priest recently asked me, "When do you feel like you can be yourself?" I was surprised at the tears that welled up in my eyes. "In the woods, when I'm alone with my Lord," I said. That wouldn't have been true twelve years ago.

Every Christian needs other Christians to point out new possibilities of faith and growth. None of us is so advanced as to be a self-sufficient "spiritual machine" that has a monopoly on the Christian life. When I read the classics, I'm challenged by the fire and holy passion burning in the souls of men and women who ached to know God as intimately as He can be known.

While our spiritual diet needs to go beyond our generation, pious readings can include modern writers. When we find someone writing today who speaks to our souls in a powerful way, we should eagerly, but wisely, consider the author's truth. Modern books are untested, but they can still be very valuable.

Practicing a Lost Art

Because reading pious works is practically a lost art, mentioning some basic practices may be helpful. *The first thing to remember is that devotional reading is not solely an intellectual exercise; its aim is the active transformation of the heart.* Dr. James Houston, professor of spirituality at Regent College, has said that most damnation comes not through ignorance but in keeping things in our heads instead of our hearts.

We read with our hearts by allowing God to challenge our attitudes, our reactions, and our emotions. We can read lists of ethical do's and don'ts while our hearts remain untouched. Devotional reading is meant to challenge the inner soul. I read systematic theology to find out how to think correctly, but I read John of the Cross to measure the temperature of my heart.

We read with the heart by reading slowly, prayerfully considering each phrase and always with a listening ear to God's Spirit. Perhaps a point will be emphasized or a Bible verse will come to mind that underscores the point's importance. This may be the Holy Spirit applying the truth we're reading to our souls.

The second thing to remember is that it's usually more profitable to read a good book two or three times than to read five mediocre books. I realize that all of us have different learning styles, but very few of us can "own" a book—in the sense that its truth becomes part of us—after one quick reading. Devotional books need to be read and reread slowly, perhaps taking as long as a year to finish one book, so that we can consider and ponder ideas and thoughts before moving on.

The third thing to remember is that, unlike scriptural reading, we need to be wary of the writer's limited perspective. William Law's later book, *The Spirit of Love,* has a considerably different emphasis than his *Serious Call.* The norm is that a writer will sound very legalistic in the early years and then in the later years mature into a more grace-filled approach stressing intimacy with God over zealous works. It helps to know where a writer is on his or her journey so you can provide a biblical balance.

The fourth thing to remember is that truth is often found in paradox.[15] Two people who disagree may both be right but emphasizing different faces of the truth. This does not mean there is not absolute truth—there is. It just means we don't always communicate truth as accurately as we might.

When we encounter spiritual writings, our tendency may be to completely reject a writer's particular emphasis rather than find the truth that his or her side represents. When I read John Climacus's account of the monastic "prison" in which very painful acts of penance are performed in a virtual torture chamber, I am horrified by the self-abuse that was carried on in the name of Christianity. I can either dismiss it out of hand and profit nothing, or I can be challenged by

---

[15]"Faith embraces many apparently contradictory truths," Pascal wrote. "The source of all heresies is the exclusion of certain of these truths" (*Pensées,* 252–53).

seeing what lengths other Christians have gone to to be rid of sin. I may disagree entirely with their method, but I can learn a great deal from their motivation.

Augustine wrote that all truth is God's truth, not meaning that every system is true, of course, but that every truth comes from God's system. The spiritual classics can't be read with the same absolute authority as Scripture, but they do contain much truth that must sometimes be filtered. Read for synthesis, not exclusion.

You'll find the makings of a suggested reading list—with some short descriptions—in the Selected Bibliography at the end of this book.

2. Imitate Living Examples

Paul endorsed the idea of human examples when he wrote, "Imitate me, just as I also imitate Christ."[16] Thomas à Kempis honored Paul's truth when he wrote, "Gather some profit to thy soul wheresoever thou art; so as if thou seest or hearest of any good examples, stir up thyself to the imitation thereof."[17]

Every human example will fall short of the example of Christ, but this is no reason to ignore the small corner of truth each of us possesses. You've probably noticed already that I often mention spiritual encounters from which I've learned something. (I also regularly "feed" from written biographies.) This book, in fact, is dedicated to Dr. Klaus Bockmuehl, whose example moved me deeply.

I want to be someone from whom others can learn; that's part of my calling as a Christian maturing in the faith. But the

[16] 1 Cor. 11:1 (NKJV). See also 1 Cor. 4:16; 1 Thess. 1:6; 2 Thess. 3:9; Phil. 3:17; Heb. 6:12 and 13:7.

[17] à Kempis, *The Imitation of Christ*, I:25:5.

process of maturity necessitates that I seek out and learn from good, positive examples. When I see people who seem to have an unusual presence of Christ in their lives, I ask them questions. I want to know how they've become what they've become.

3. Cultivate Virtues

True virtue isn't an achievement as much as it is a gift, the fruit of the Spirit. But the ancients—and Scripture—agree that we can and should cooperate with the Spirit's work.

Teresa of Avila encouraged her sisters, "It is necessary that your foundation consist of more than prayer and contemplation. If you do not strive for the virtues and practice them, you will always be dwarfs. And, please God, it will be only a matter of not growing, for you already know that whoever does not increase decreases. I hold that love, where present, cannot possibly be content with remaining always the same."[18]

The art of cultivating virtue little by little is being recovered somewhat by the home-schooling movement as parents seek to train their children to become patient, kind, honest, and hardworking, among other things. We would all do well, however, to heed the principle understood by these parents that virtues don't come by accident. They require a conscious effort on our part. "At the beginning of our religious life, we cultivate the virtues, and we do so with toil and difficulty."[19]

Spiritual training assumes we can change—that the lazy can, in cooperation with the Spirit's work, become diligent, the selfish can learn to love, and the cruel can learn to be

[18]Teresa of Avila, *The Interior Castle*, trans. Kieran Kavanaugh and Otilio Rodriguez (New York: Paulist Press, 1979), VII:4:9.

[19]Climacus, *The Ladder of Divine Ascent*, 77.

kind. We needn't see ourselves as slaves to the darker sides of our personalities.

Not everyone has the same obstacles to overcome in the cultivation of virtues. Some of us may have great discipline but struggle against selfish ambition. Others may be very gentle but avoid conflict at all costs. Some of us have a natural temper while others tend toward greater sensuality. All these problems can be overcome, but just as a natural athlete can be defeated by a less gifted athlete who trains harder, so more naturally virtuous people can be overcome by others who apply themselves more seriously to growth. Thomas à Kempis wrote, "All men have not equally much to overcome and mortify. Yet he that is diligent, though he have more passions, shall profit more in virtue, than another that is of a more temperate disposition, if he is less fervent in the pursuit of virtue."[20]

Cultivating virtues is a necessary part of the Christian life. "That's just the way I am" is a confession of sloth, not humility. It's admitting that we are too spiritually lazy to change, too selfishly indifferent to how our weaknesses and our lack of virtue create casualties. Whether it's a bad temper or an overly indulgent lifestyle, others are affected.

4. Use Discomfort

A fourth aspect of training requires us to overcome our reluctance to any sort of discomfort. As sinful people, we are naturally inclined toward ease, comfort, and self-assertion. Training can be painful, and pain is a price that many of us simply are not willing to pay.

We naturally indulge ourselves, which, on occasion, can be

[20] à Kempis, *The Imitation of Christ*, I:25:4.

healthy, but if we're not watchful, these self-indulgences can make us soft. That's why John Climacus urged us to fight "spiritual descent" by cultivating rather than serving our inclinations.

> Endeavor to be inclined always:
> not to the easiest, but to the most difficult;
> not to the most delightful, but to the harshest;
> not to the most gratifying, but to the less pleasant;
> not to what means rest for you, but to hard work;
> not to the consoling, but to the unconsoling;
> not to the most, but to the least;
> not to the highest and most precious, but to the lowest and most despised;
> not to wanting something, but to wanting nothing;
> do not go about looking for the best of temporal things, but for the worst. . . .

> You should embrace these practices earnestly and try to overcome the repugnance of your will toward them. If you sincerely put them into practice with order and discretion, you will discover in them great delight and consolation.[21]

Notice that John Climacus urged us to "endeavor to be inclined. . . ." *Endeavor* means to strive, to work toward an end, to cultivate what isn't already there. We can shape our passions and habits by training and by not always choosing the easy or the comfortable road. The little decisions we make about how to spend our time and what to eat are really spiritual battles through which our characters are shaped.

Discomfort can be a friend, not a foe, for those who truly

[21]Climacus, *The Ladder of Divine Ascent*, 77–78.

want to grow. (We'll discuss this in greater depth in chapter nine.)

5. *Practice Holiness*

Ultimately, training points toward incarnating the truth in our lives, and that means living out the truth and God's call to holiness in our bodies. The body, however, is often our biggest hindrance to training. Jesus warned the disciples that "the spirit indeed is willing, but the flesh is weak" (Matt. 26:41 NKJV), and Paul painfully lived in this reality: "For I delight in the law of God according to the inward man. But I see another law in my members, warring against the law of my mind, and bringing me into captivity to the law of sin which is in my members" (Rom. 7:22–23 NKJV).

Any spiritual training, then, that neglects the body neglects the one area that really matters.[22] This is not to forget the very real danger of legalism; merely acting right in the body doesn't cleanse our hearts. The threat of legalism, though, shouldn't hold us back from training to see the truth lived out in our bodies.

Giving way to our bodies keeps us from giving way to God. William Law told us that training our bodies is thus essential to building a life of holiness: "Since we are neither all soul nor all body, seeing none of our actions are either separately of the soul or separately of the body, seeing we have no habits but such as are produced by the actions both of our souls and bodies, it is certain that if we would arrive at habits of devotion or delight in God, we must not only meditate and exercise

---

[22]This, of course, was the failing of the gnostics, who believed that as long as they were spiritually pure, what they did with their bodies didn't matter. A modern-day counterpart might be that as long as we have prayed the sinner's prayer, all our physical actions don't matter.

our souls, but we must practice and exercise our bodies to all such outward actions as are conformable to these inward tempers."[23]

Though actions cannot make us right with God, and though it is important that we don't have a disconnection between our hearts and our actions, it is still true that by governing our actions we can govern our hearts. Law said, "As we are masters of our outward actions; as we can force ourselves to outward acts of reading, praying, singing, and the like; and as all these bodily actions have an effect upon the soul as they naturally tend to form such and such tempers in our hearts; by being masters of these outward, bodily actions, we have great power over the inward state of our heart."[24]

The body can be our friend or our foe, depending on whether we master it or it masters us. The ultimate issue for me has been: Will I always give in to my body's desires, or will I govern my body and decide to give it only what it needs? William Law urged us to consider our bodies as "the servant and minister of our soul," and this thought has been very helpful to me.[25]

The opposing danger, of course, is to focus so much on the body that it becomes an end in itself. This must be rejected as strongly. Certainly, the spirit of this age tends to make us more concerned about crafting a fine physique than building a soul that is presentable to God, which, in light of eternity, and even temporal history (bodies must, after all, grow old and then decay), is really quite shortsighted. Law warned us,

[23]Law, *A Serious Call*, 216–17.

[24]Ibid., 216.

[25]"Consider your body only as the servant and minister of your soul; and only so nourish it as it may best perform a humble and obedient service to it" (Law, *A Serious Call*, 259).

"As to your bodies, you are to consider them as poor, perishing things that are sickly and corrupt at present and will soon drop into common dust. . . . whenever you are more intent upon adorning your persons than upon the perfecting of your souls, you are much more beside yourselves than he that had rather have a laced coat than a healthful body."[26]

One quick caution is in order at this point. Though we train our bodies and souls, our faith is not rooted in them but in Christ's death and resurrection. We need to guard against despair when we do poorly, remembering that Christ's work on the cross covers us, and, likewise, we need to avoid pride when we do well, remembering that God's Spirit sustains us. The center of our spiritual lives must always rest in God and what He has done, not in our experiential faith.

6. Early Rising

An additional element of training in the spiritual life (to the despairing cry of many) is that there is something sacred about the early side of morning. It has become an important part of my life to "awaken the morning" by rising before dawn. Early rising historically has been an important part of Christian spiritual training. William Law wrote:

I take it for granted that every Christian that is in health is up early in the morning; for it is much more reasonable to suppose a person up early because he is a Christian than because he is a laborer, or a tradesman, or a servant, or has business that wants him.

We naturally conceive some abhorrence of a man that is in bed when he should be at his labor or in his shop. We can't tell

[26]Law, *A Serious Call*, 270–71.

how to think anything fond of him who is such a slave to drowsiness as to neglect his business for it.

Let this therefore teach us to conceive how odious we must appear in the sight of Heaven if we are in bed shut up in sleep and darkness, when we should be praising God, and are such slaves to drowsiness as to neglect our devotions for it.[27]

Training involves more than finding helpful teaching, more than setting realistic goals for steady results, more than accepting the pain, more than disciplining the body. It also involves setting the right schedule. There is a style of life generally consistent with those who cultivate spiritual growth and a style of life generally consistent with those who wouldn't know a spiritual thought unless it bit them in bodily form.

Common sense confirms that what the ancients advised is good: In the long run, those who keep later hours are generally going to be less efficient. Those who choose to sleep late lose the best hours of the day.

Rising early is about more than efficiency, however. A moral element is involved. As a sin-laden man living in a sinful world, I've found I'm much more vulnerable to particular types of sin after 9 P.M. than I am when I arise at 5 A.M., except, perhaps, for attitudinal sins like the slavish pursuit of money or selfish ambition.

Therefore, as my schedule evolved into rising at 5 A.M. or even earlier, my opportunities and inclinations toward certain sins were not half as numerous as they were before. And as I disciple others, especially younger men, I've noticed that many of the most troublesome difficulties occur in the late evening. A disciplined schedule can actually cut the opportunity to sin—and, therefore, help cut the place of sin in our hearts and lives.

[27]Ibid., 189.

Early rising does more than guard us from excessive temptation, however. It also guards us against overindulgence in sleep itself, which can have a slow but steady and debilitating influence on the Christian life. William Law wrote, "Now this is the case of those who waste their time in sleep; it does not disorder their lives or wound their consciences as notorious acts of intemperance do; but like any other more moderate course of indulgence, it silently and by smaller degrees wears away the spirit of religion and sinks the soul into a state of dullness and sensuality."[28] Rising early, then, is about more than creating time in our schedule. According to Law, overindulgence in sleep "gives a softness and idleness to your soul, and is so contrary to that lively, zealous, watchful, self-denying spirit which was not only the Spirit of Christ and His Apostles, the spirit of all the Saints and martyrs which have ever been amongst men, but must be the spirit of all those who would not sink in the common corruption of the world."[29]

There is also something about morning that calls us to prayer. Seeing the sun appear lifts our spirits to God, breaking us into thanksgiving. If your prayers have become rote recitations of intercession, you're probably praying two or three hours too late. Get up earlier and just try not to worship. It's a very difficult thing to do! After all, even common sense tells us we do best to sleep when temptation is at its highest and arise when our spiritual faculties are at their highest.

7. Living a Life of Reflection
Scripture's call to actively pursue training in godliness (1 Tim. 4:7) presupposes some times of reflection to deter-

[28]Ibid., 192.
[29]Ibid., 195.

mine how we have progressed or fallen short. I know almost nothing about weight rooms except that every one I've been in has large mirrors that allow the athletes to examine their bodies and notice their progress. Selfish preoccupation is death to a growing spirituality, but sensible reflection is an essential and healthy element of Christianity—a mirror held up to our spiritual progress. If we never take stock of where we are, years can fly by without any advantage being gained from them.

Thomas à Kempis urged us to view life as a journey, with heaven as our destination; each new season is another step in our travels, and we can use it to make sure we're headed in the right direction. "From festival to festival, we should make some good resolution, as though we were then to depart out of this world, and to come to the everlasting feast in heaven. Therefore ought we carefully to prepare ourselves at holy times, and to live more devoutly, and to keep more strictly all things that we are to observe, as though we were shortly at God's hands to receive the reward of our labors."[30]

Through the years Christians have used various means of reflections, including journaling, confession, or even a spiritual program such as Teresa of Avila's seven dwelling places or John Climacus's thirty steps on the ladder of divine ascent. William Law practiced a time of reflection *every evening*, examining how he had done in light of his spiritual goals. I have found birthdays to be an ideal time to reflect at length on my life's calling and spiritual growth. As I do this, I have been able to see particular weaknesses—such as an overly sensitive conscience—gradually transformed. That gives me hope that

[30]à Kempis, *The Imitation of Christ*, I:19:6.

current weaknesses—a propensity toward fear, for example—will also be transformed.

It's exciting to see a weakness torn out or a strength strongly planted in a moment of exhilarating prayer; but most often, God brings virtues out of us like a plant out of the ground. First there's a small stalk of green, then the separate leaves, and finally the flowers. Reflection reminds us that growth is a process that keeps us from growing lazy and keeps our hope alive when growth seems delayed.

Regular reflection keeps the years from slipping by, unappreciated; I taste every one. I will not pass into eternity without having given this life—what it means, how to live it, what needs to be done—much thought. This, too, I consider a gift given to me through the wisdom of the communion of saints.

Learning to Live with Grace

Discussing training in the Christian life is potentially dangerous. For those who understand it, in context, training is a feast from the ancients. For those who tend toward legalism, it's a dangerous prescription that could be poisonous if taken in the wrong manner. Still, the concept of rigorous training in the spiritual life is so historically established that one can scarcely discuss Christian spirituality without mentioning it, even at the risk of leading some people to become legalists who respond to guilt. Christian spirituality is a spirituality of grace in which an awakened heart responds to God's mercy by giving all. We bring nothing to God, and He gives us everything.

A righteous life and rigorous training without a heart full of grace is like an egg without a yolk—a fragile shell that will break under the slightest pressure. Not only are Pharisees a bore and an active bother, they eventually crack under the strain of impossible expectations.

That is only one side of the truth, however, for though Pharisees are eggs without yolks, those who try to exist solely on mercy without structure or discipline are like eggs without shells—a sticky, gooey mess.

Legalism, on the one hand, and complacency, on the other, are twin enemies to true Christian spirituality. Paul spoke scathingly of anyone who added a milligram to grace, but he could scarcely mention the word without adding, in essence, "But we don't continue to live the way we used to."[31]

In all our efforts—setting the right schedule, obtaining the right teaching, cultivating the right virtue, and so on—we mustn't forget the covering of grace. Some of us will try to do too much too soon. Brother Lawrence warned of a woman who "wants to go faster than grace. One does not become holy all at once."[32] John Climacus cautioned his readers: "The fact is that no one can climb a ladder in a single stride."[33] He added, "at the beginning of one's life as a monk one cannot suddenly become free of gluttony and vainglory."[34]

William Law, our champion of training in the spiritual life, stressed the importance of laboring *with the right spirit*. His strict writings, he said, were "not intended to possess people's minds with a scrupulous anxiety and discontent in the service of God, but to fill them with a just fear of living in sloth and idleness and in the neglect of such virtues as they

[31]See Rom. 5:20—6:2.

[32]Brother Lawrence, *The Practice of the Presence of God*, Tenth Letter, 28 March 1689 (Cincinnati: Forward Movement Publications).

[33]Climacus, *The Ladder of Divine Ascent*, 225.

[34]Ibid., 254.

will want at the day of judgment. It is to excite them to an earnest examination of their lives, to such zeal and care and concern after Christian perfection as they use in any matter that has gained their heart and affections."[35]

Responsibility and grace are the twin pillars that support the foundation of the Christian life. At times, we will be tempted to shirk responsibility. At other times, we may forget about grace. The latter is as much a temptation as the former.

Francis de Sales reminds us that "it is necessary sometimes to relax our minds, as well as our bodies, by some kind of recreation."[36] God is the pilot of our salvation; He can cause us to grow "even while we sleep." Rest, spiritual and otherwise, is part of the spiritual process, even to the point of being encased in the Ten Commandments through the call to keep the Sabbath.

This is a good place to complete this discussion, for the Sabbath commandment contains the balance so necessary to a healthy Christian life. The Sabbath contains two elements: the call to work, "Six days you shall labor and do all your work," and the call to rest, "but the seventh day. . . . you shall do no work" (Exod. 20:9–10 NKJV).

The problem with so many of us is that we don't labor during the six days and we don't rest during the seventh. We live in the gray wasteland of killing time, which is neither restful nor productive. Thus we feel unable to keep one day devoted to rest because we failed to fill the previous six days with work.

As fallen men and women, we can only progress so far, but we can progress. That's the tension. As Law wrote, "We

[35]Law, *A Serious Call*, 68.

[36]Francis de Sales, *Introduction to a Devout Life* (Rome: Frederick Pustet and Co., n.d.), 241.

cannot offer to God the service of angels; we cannot obey Him as man in a state of perfection could; but fallen men can do their best, and this is the perfection required of us."[37]

Reflections

Read Matthew 5:1–12. Have you ever consciously applied yourself to incarnating the beatitudes into your life?

Galatians 5:19–26 tells us what to avoid and what to become. Pray over the list—what is God asking you to do in this moment? How can you train yourself to be godly?

Pick the area covered in this chapter where you feel weakest—whether it's pious reading, learning from a good example, cultivating virtue, living a life of reflection, accepting discomfort, incarnating the truth in your body, or waking up early. Which area is God leading you to concentrate on first? What steps can you take to obey?

[37]Law, *A Serious Call*, 67.

Chapter Four

Holiness of the Heart:
Avoiding Sin and Temptation

> *When one is already leading an honest and regulated life, it is far more important, in order to become a true Christian, to change the within rather than the without.*
>
> Fénelon
>
> *We have established and developed . . . admirable rules of polity, ethics and justice, but at root, the evil root of man, this evil stuff of which we are made is only concealed; it is not pulled up.*   Pascal

Near the seminary I attended was a small convenience store where we often went for study breaks. One of the walls of the convenience store was full of magazines—some of them pornographic. We'd go from hearing about an exciting moment in church history, or perhaps one of Packer's lectures on the book of Romans—the high, lofty, and holy—and be reminded as we bought our snacks and drinks of the low, often perverted baseness of the real world.

It was a curious sensation for me when my heart started acting differently in that store. As a single man going to college, I had never even thought about pornography. It wasn't that I was victorious over temptation, it was just that I had never really faced the temptation. Now here I was, a married man going to seminary, and my heart would start to flutter as I passed by those magazines.

One afternoon the temptation became acute. It was a tense period in the school year; finances were so tight that I wasn't sure if I'd even be able to continue going to school, and "that store" seemed to be yelling out my name. Unwisely, I didn't dismiss the temptation; I just put it off as an irritant. That did nothing to kill it or lessen it, however, and it stayed with me most of the day. Classes helped to keep my mind occupied, but when they were over and the day's structure was removed, I was amazed by how much the temptation seized me.

What was the turning point for me? I'm not sure—if I could bottle it for future use, I would—but somehow God broke through and I said a loud and final "No!" I knew at that moment even if that store was the last place on earth where I could get something to drink, I wouldn't go in it, at least not that afternoon.

The temptation was over.

End of story, you might think—but not quite. Driving home, I felt pretty satisfied with myself. I had faced temptation, and I had won! I even began to think of ways I could work my victory into a sermon illustration. And then, as I was driving along, the Lord's voice swiftly cut me down. I almost had to pull over.

God tore away the veil of my heart and showed me the evil within it. I had avoided one sin only to fall into another—self-righteous pride. As I recounted it to a fellow seminarian, I remarked that instead of going from "strength to strength," as Scripture mentions, I was living from "sin to sin."

It was a frustrating recognition. If I faced a temptation, I could give in and that would be a sin, or I could not give in, become proud, and still end up sinning. How could I win?

I had to learn that in one sense, I couldn't win. My problem was that I was making myself, my actions, my thoughts, and my attitudes the measurement of my faith. The holiness God wants is a holiness rooted in Christ's death and resurrection, a holiness that changes our hearts, not just our actions.

That day I began to be liberated from the crushing burden of believing I had to become the holiest man who ever lived. I still don't want sin to have any place in my life, but the burden of striving has been replaced with a desire to know God in an ever more intimate way so that I don't sin simply because I no longer want to sin. In the words of Francis de Sales, I had to learn that "obedience must rather be loved than disobedience feared."

I also learned, however, that even when I gain mastery over bodily sins—something that will never be complete this side of heaven—God is still concerned about my internal world and the status of my heart and attitudes.

As I read the classics and the stories of their authors, I am encouraged by their honest approach to sin, holiness, and temptation. We'll be quoting several authors in this chapter, but you'll notice in particular the work of three. I've chosen two who focus on building a holiness of the heart—Francis de Salignac de La Mothe Fénelon (who, with your pardon, we'll refer to simply as Fénelon) and Francis de Sales—and one who focuses on a very practical and disciplined approach, William Law. These authors can lead the way toward a very practical and heartfelt Christian holiness.

The Teachers of Holiness

Fénelon, a seventeenth-century mystic,[1] was well known as a skilled spiritual counselor. He soon found himself charged with educating and reforming Louis XIV's grandson, the duke of Burgandy. This might at first sound like a great honor—and in truth it was—but it was also a great challenge. The young duke was described by a contemporary as "born terrible, and in his early youth he made everyone tremble. Hard and irascible to the utmost passion, incapable of bearing the slightest resistance without flying into a rage . . . obstinate . . . passionately fond of every kind of pleasure."[2]

Modern wisdom might tell us to send such a youth to military training and let strict discipline bring his life into order. Fénelon, however, pursued a different approach. He was gentle, believing that a teacher must "mingle teaching and play; let wisdom show herself to the child only at intervals, and with a smiling face. If he forms a sad and gloomy conception of virtue, all is lost."[3]

Fénelon's method must have worked, for the same person who gave us the earlier description of the duke described the transformation this way: "The marvel is that in a very short space of time, devotion and grace made quite another being of him, and changed his many and dreadful faults into the

---

[1]The word *mystic* has often caused great concern to many Christians because it sounds like something occultic. Certainly there are occultic mystics, but historically and academically the word has also been used to describe Christians who seek a direct experience of God. Whenever a Christian says he or she wants to know God, not just know about Him, this person is, to various degrees, approaching the world of a Christian mystic.

[2]Paul Janet, *Fénelon: His Life and Works*, trans. Victor Leuliette (Port Washington, NY: Kennikat Press, 1970), 47.

[3]Ibid., 28–29.

entirely opposite virtues. From this abyss a Prince was seen to issue, at once affable, gentle, humane, generous, patient, modest, humble, and severe towards himself."[4]

In the midst of his call to reform others, Fénelon remained very much aware of his own failings. The man who offered so much spiritual advice to others wrote of himself, "I am to myself . . . the whole of a great diocese, more burdensome than the outside one, and a diocese which I am incapable of reforming."[5]

Francis de Sales was also a noted spiritual adviser in his day. Though having lived a fairly pious life, de Sales admitted that the two most difficult passions for him were love and anger. He once said to his friend Jeanne Chantal, "There is not a soul in the world, I think, who loves more cordially, tenderly, and so to say more amorously than I."[6]

Yet de Sales was still able to have real, deep, and meaningful relationships with others—including available women—without falling into sin, because he learned the art of diversion, transforming a worldly passion into love of God.

Because de Sales was aware of his own temptations, he was able to be gentle (rather than afraid) of the temptations of others. He wrote, "I have never allowed myself to give way to anger or reproach without repenting of it; if I have had the happiness of reclaiming heretics, it has been by gentleness. Love is a stronger power over souls."[7]

When Fénelon and de Sales speak to us, then, we know they are men who worked with real people in real-life situa-

[4]Ibid., 48.

[5]Ibid., 235.

[6]Louis Sempe, *St. Francis de Sales* (Milwaukee: Bruce Publishing, 1933), 20.

[7]Katherine Bregy, *The Story of Saint Francis de Sales* (Milwaukee: Bruce Publishing, 1958), 36.

tions. They were aware of the sin in their own hearts, yet they found a way to live lives worthy of emulation. Let's see what they, and others, have discovered.

In Search of Holy Holiness

As we seek a holy holiness, we must first understand the absurdity of sin and move on to a discussion of what holiness is and is not. Armed with this knowledge, we will then explore what the ancients urged us to do when temptation strikes. Next we will learn how to make sin our servant, grow with gentleness, and avoid the trap of soul sadness.

The Absurdity of Sin

Our quest to understand holiness begins with understanding the absurdity of sin. Fénelon pointed out that sin is self-defeating. "We refuse ourselves to God, who only wants to save us. We give ourselves up to the world, which only wants us to tyrannize over us and destroy us."[8]

A performance-based Christian says, "I want to do this, but I know I shouldn't. I must either find a way to not do this or to not get caught." The relation-based Christian asks, "Who do I want to be in love with? My Lord or this sin?"

Merely asking ourselves this question unmasks the ugliness of sin. Sin creates massive disturbances in our lives; holiness brings peace. When we look honestly at what each brings, we have to ask ourselves, why, indeed, this sin is even tempting us. This is where the writings of William Law add to our discussion. He wrote, "These passions are the causes of all the disquiets and vexations of human life. They are the

[8]Fénelon, *Christian Perfection*, 40.

dropsies and fevers of our minds, vexing them with false appetites and restless cravings after such things as we do not want, and spoiling our taste for those things which are our proper good."[9]

Christianity, with its moral calling, may seem repressive to the world, but when we see sin as it really is (slow suicide), the moral calling of Christianity takes on a whole new light. William Law put it best when he wrote, "Surely it can be no uncomfortable state of life to be rescued by religion from such self-murder and to be rendered capable of eternal happiness."[10]

Any other way of living "is living wholly against ourselves and will end in our own shame and confusion of face."[11] Sin in this sense is nothing but self-abuse.

While some would call themselves free of the restraints of Christianity, Law saw it another way. "They may live a while free from the restraints and directions of religion, but instead thereof they must be under the absurd government of their passions."[12] And our passions, as any thoughtful Christian knows, are harder taskmasters than is our God of mercy and grace.

A life dedicated to holiness, in this sense, is actually self-serving[13]—but it's self-serving as it first affirms God's order and purpose of Creation. In this it's pleasing to God and

[9]Law, *A Serious Call*, 149.

[10]Ibid., 155. Compare with Augustine's statement, "The soul lives by avoiding what it dies by affecting" (*Confessions*, XIII:30).

[11]Law, *A Serious Call*, 158.

[12]Ibid., 160.

[13]"And thus it is in every virtue; you act up the every degree of it, the more happiness you have from it. And so of every vice: if you only abate its excesses, you do but little for yourself; but if you reject it in all degrees, then you feel the true ease and joy of a reformed mind" (Law, *A Serious Call*, 154).

ultimately pleasing to ourselves. That's why the ancients viewed sin as so absurd. Sin is not inviting but debilitating; holiness is not burdensome but liberating. Law explained, "By these rules we change the childish satisfactions of our vain and sickly passions for the solid enjoyments and real happiness of a sound mind."[14] Even when we understand that sin is absurd, temptation will still strike and we'll still hesitate.

What Holiness Is

What is the basis of holiness? The ancients, beginning with Jesus and Paul, agreed that holiness was not a question of purity overcoming passion but of transforming passion into purity's service.

When we talk of holiness, we must be very explicit about what we mean, for as Pascal warns, "experience shows us an enormous difference between piety and goodness."[15] Perhaps you've noticed this difference in your interaction with other Christians. We feel God's redeeming love and grace when we get together with some believers. Their holiness is a warm hearth, a shelter that invites us to come in from the cold. Even though we sense an underlying strength that tells us sin and manipulation are not acceptable in their presence—and this can be somewhat fearful—we still find ourselves drawn to them.

There are others whose holiness seems to be a prison. It is forced, uncomfortable, and ragged at the edges. The biting edge of accusation and judgment pushes us away from them. When they talk about sin, their voices seem marked by fear, not understanding or wisdom.

[14]Law, *A Serious Call*, 148.
[15]Pascal, *Pensées*, 135.

The spiritual fathers taught that true holiness has at its root an overwhelming passion for the one true and holy God, not for rules, principles, or standards. This holiness is relational. Fénelon wrote, "It is not by fussiness that we become faithful and exact in the smallest things. It is by a feeling of love, which is free from the reflections and fears of the anxious and scrupulous. We are as though carried away by the love of God. We only want to do what we are doing, and we do not want to do anything at all which we are not doing. At the same time that God, jealous, urges the soul, presses it relentlessly in the least details, and seems to withdraw all liberty from it, it finds itself free, and it enjoys a profound peace in him."[16]

Teresa of Avila joined Fénelon in this understanding of a relational holiness that results from drawing near to God and having our appetites transformed: "[the soul] has already experienced spiritual delight from God, it sees that worldly delights are like filth. It finds itself withdrawing from them little by little, and it is more master of itself for so doing. In sum, there is an improvement in all the virtues."[17]

Most of us want to be rid of our longstanding sins in a day. We think that by praying, "I'll never do it again!" we can somehow shout ourselves out of years of habitual failure. Holy holiness focuses on drawing near to God. As the love of God fills our heart, the desire for sin is cut off and dies like a withering plant that never gets watered; but this is a process, not an overnight experience. Stress, confusion, weariness— any number of things—can resurrect the old habits of relating.

[16]Francois Fénelon, *Christian Perfection*, trans. Mildred Whitney Stillman (Minneapolis: Bethany House, 1975), 35.

[17]Teresa of Avila, *The Interior Castle*, VII:3:9.

That is why we must continually apply ourselves anew to loving God.

When we yearn for our Creator "as the deer pants for the water" (Ps. 42:1), when we learn to love the Lord our God with all our heart, soul, mind, and strength (Mark 12:30) then holiness will be the by-product of our passion. We cease from sin, not just because we are disciplined, but because we have found something better. This doesn't mean principles can't serve us; it does mean principles can't save us.

Yet our outward actions, at their best, are imperfect pictures of the state of our hearts; it is possible to do everything right and still be 99 percent hypocrite.

What Holiness Isn't

"We do not keep ourselves virtuous by our own power," Pascal wrote, "but by the counterbalance of two opposing vices, just as we stay upright between two contrary winds. Take one of these vices away and we fall into the other."[18]

What did Pascal mean by this? A man or woman who works very hard may simply be avoiding the sin of laziness by being filled with selfish ambition or greed. Remove his or her hunger for more money, and this person will immediately become as lazy as any of us.

Others might be very disciplined around food. They would be the last persons on earth you would label as gluttons. Yet they are disciplined around food because they want to have a physique that will draw attention to themselves, not because they don't want food to have a hold on their hearts and steal their affection for God. They may be free from gluttony only because they are slaves to vanity.

[18]Pascal, *Pensées*, 242.

Do you see how we play vice against vice—using vanity to destroy gluttony, for instance—and are upheld by the struggle of two sins? This is a much different holiness than the ancients' view of a transforming passion that gives birth to virtue. On and on we could go, showing how 90 percent of our virtue is a sham, a vice wearing a coat and tie. That's why Jesus constantly pointed us to the heart, the one battlefield that really matters. The state of our heart is the true state of our virtue.[19]

When Temptation Strikes

A growing holiness will reduce certain temptations, and sin may have to find more subtle ways to attack us. None of us, however, will become so mature that we will not, at times, be looking temptation in the face. How did the ancients say we should respond?

Again, a holy passion for God is the primary antidote. Consistently, we are told to run, as a little child would run, into the Father's arms. Fénelon taught that we should act like a small child who, when shown something horrible, "only recoils from it and buries himself in his mother's breast, so that he will see nothing. The practice of the presence of God is the supreme remedy. It sustains. It comforts. It calms."[20]

Francis de Sales similarly advised:

As soon as you perceive yourself tempted, follow the example of children when they see a wolf or a bear in the country; for they immediately run into the arms of their father or mother, or at

[19]"Many an action which in men's sight is disapproved, is by Thy testimony approved; and many, by men praised, are (Thou being witness) condemned: because the show of the action, and the mind of the doer, and the unknown exigency of the period, severally vary" Augustine, *Confessions*, III.17.

[20]Fénelon, *Christian Perfection*, 24.

least they call out to them for help or assistance. It is the remedy which our Lord has taught: "Pray, that ye enter not into temptation" Matt. 26:41 [KJV].

If you find that the temptation, nevertheless, still continues, or even increases, run in spirit to embrace the holy cross, as if you saw our Savior Jesus Christ crucified before you. Protest that you never will consent to the temptation, implore his assistance against it, and still refuse your consent as long as the temptation shall continue.

But, in making these protestations and refusals of consent, look not the temptation in the face, but look only on our Lord. . . . Divert your thoughts to some good and pious reflections, for, when good thoughts occupy your heart, they will drive away every temptation and suggestion.[21]

What we don't want to do is arrogantly try and fight a stronger foe. John Climacus warned, "Do not imagine that you will overwhelm the demon of fornication by entering into an argument with him. Nature is on his side and he has the best of the argument. So the man who decides to struggle against his flesh and to overcome it by his own efforts is fighting in vain. . . . Offer up to the Lord the weakness of your nature. Admit your incapacity and, without your knowing it, you will win for yourself the gift of chastity."[22]

We will learn, in time, when to fight and when to flee. There is a place, as the great Puritan scholar John Owen said, to "mortify" (put to death) sin. But mortification is often best done before temptation strikes. Once it is upon us, we need to be wise. John Climacus admonished, "We must be very shrewd in the matter of knowing when to stand up against

[21]de Sales, *Introduction to a Devout Life*, 299.
[22]Climacus, *The Ladder of Divine Ascent*, 173.

sin, when and to what extent to fight against whatever nourishes the passions, and when to withdraw from the struggle. Because of our weakness there are times when we must choose flight if we are to avoid death."[23]

Focusing on sin, either by committing it or by being consumed with fighting it, keeps us from practicing God's presence. God forbid that we should ever define ourselves or our days solely by what we *didn't* do. Let us instead be people who define ourselves by practicing God's presence. Let us use temptation to remind us to think of Him, our soul's true delight.

Making Sin Our Servant

It would be heresy to suggest that we should ever sin so we can grow. Sin is always the wrong choice. However, when we do sin, we might as well cooperate with God in learning a lesson from our fall so we don't repeat it. Genuine repentance renews the soul like few other activities and places us in a posture of learning.

Fénelon wrote, "The sin seems hideous, but the humiliation which comes from it, and for which God has permitted it, seems good. As the reflections of pride about our own faults are bitter, worried and chagrined, so the return of the soul to God after its faults is recollected, peaceful, and sustained by confidence."[24]

At some stages of the Christian life, we may actually feel closest to God right after we've blown it and met Him in repentance. This is because our pride, so odious to God and so ignored by us, is finally broken by sin and even at times

[23]Ibid., 255.
[24]Fénelon, *Christian Perfection*, 97.

by temptation. Fénelon continued, "Thou allowest a mixture of good and evil even in the hearts of those who are most devoted to thee. These imperfections which remain in good souls serve to humble them, to detach them from themselves, to make them feel their own weakness, to make them run more eagerly to thee."[25]

Thomas à Kempis found great potential for growth in temptation. "Temptations are often very profitable to us, though they be troublesome and grievous; for in them a man is humbled, purified, and instructed."[26]

He added later, "Wherefore to many it is more profitable not to be altogether free from temptations, but to be often assaulted, lest they should be too secure, and so perhaps be puffed up with pride; or else too freely give themselves to worldly comforts."[27]

But how desperately we want to be free from these temptations! There is one in particular I have wanted God to remove. My "thorn in the flesh" when it comes to relationships is a reluctance to speak the hard word of truth. I want to be liked. As the third of four children, perhaps I was born into (and have since fostered) the unfortunate role of being a people-pleaser.

People ask my opinion, and I am always tempted to round the edges of truth. Sometimes, I have even lied. One person showed me some artwork he had designed. He asked me, "Does this look homemade and unprofessional?" It was a miserable piece of art and a clear-cut temptation. Unfortunately, I replied "No." I lacked the courage to stand up to the temptation.

[25]Ibid., 127.
[26]à Kempis, *The Imitation of Christ*, I:13:2.
[27]Ibid., I:20:4.

I have prayed for God to take this temptation away. When people hear me speak, I want them to know they are receiving the truth, even if the truth will make them uncomfortable.

I can examine this temptation from every angle and see how silly it is. People will actually respect and like me more in the long run if I'm absolutely honest. But I often lack the courage to face short-term difficulty for this long-term gain. I wish there were a button I could push or a prayer I could recite that would remove this failing forever. But there isn't, and I still struggle.

But you know what? This weakness keeps me close to God, especially when I'm counseling or being asked for advice. I would definitely be a better person without this sin, but would I be a better person without this temptation? I don't know. The existence of the temptation has forced me to clothe myself with humility, which is not a bad coat to wear when talking to anybody.

After we sin, rather than make promises to God that we are almost certain to break ("I promise I'll tell the truth next time, God; I really will!"), we should respond by humbly asking the right questions. Francis de Sales wrote, "Content not yourself with confessing your . . . sins, merely as to the fact, but accuse yourself also of the motive that induced you to commit them."[28]

I have had to ask myself, "Why is it hard for me to speak the truth?" That question led me to see that I want to be liked. The next question to ask was obvious—Why do I value being liked more than being honest? I'm still answering that one; but even though I hate the sin, it has opened the door to my heart so that I could confront some long-neglected

[28]de Sales, *Introduction to a Devout Life*, 107.

motivations. Every time I fail, if I ask the right questions, I learn something new. God can use my strengths to help me grow, but He can also use my weaknesses. God's ability to use even rebellion for His benefit is one of the more profound realities of His sovereignty and Lordship.

It is particularly helpful to discuss the motives of our sins. Francis de Sales counseled, "But the sovereign remedy against all temptations, whether great or small, is to lay open your heart, and communicate its suggestions, feelings, and affections to your director; for you must observe, that the first condition that the enemy of salvation makes with a soul which he desires to seduce is to keep silence. . . . whereas God, on the other hand, by his inspirations, requires that we should make them known to our superiors and directors."[29]

Living by grace does not mean living by spiritual laziness. We don't continually berate ourselves about committing the sin, but we do try, in a spirit of freedom and without overdue introspection, to discern the cause of the sin and the reason it has a motivating power in our life.

Consistent Climbing

One of the dangers of talking about holiness is that some of the more zealous among us will overdo it, wanting to progress from being the young and lusty Augustine to the mature bishop in the course of a year or even a week. Perhaps we've heard about the asceticism and harsh measures of the desert fathers. Yet we would do well to recognize that in addition to the desert fathers, there is also a strong tradition of *gentle* and *consistent* progress in holiness. Fénelon gave a warning worth heeding:

[29]de Sales, *Introduction to a Devout Life*, 300.

Most people, when they wish to be converted or reformed, expect to fill their lives with especially difficult and unusual acts, far more than to purify their intentions, and to mortify their natural inclinations in the most usual acts of their condition. In this they often badly deceive themselves. It would be much more valuable for them to change their actions less, and to change more rather the disposition which makes them act. When one is already leading an honest and regulated life, it is far more important, in order to become a true Christian, to change the within rather than the without.[30]

We are far better off keeping a constant and steady vigilance in the small things, rather than trying to prove heroic in the big things. Holiness is not something obtained between Tuesday and Wednesday, but rather the fruit of a life lived consistently and thoughtfully over the course of years and decades. "A continual and moderate sobriety is preferable to violent abstinences, practiced occasionally, and mingled with great relaxations. A moderate use of discipline awakens the appetite of devotion," Francis de Sales wrote.[31]

The "heroic plan" of holiness often tries to pour in the holiness as quickly as possible, but it ignores the millions of tiny holes that drain us dry. De Sales explained:

Wolves and bears are certainly more dangerous than fleas; yet the former neither give us so much trouble, nor exercise our patience so much, as the latter. It is easy to abstain from murder, but it is extremely difficult to restrain all the little sallies of passion, the occasions of which present themselves every moment. It is very easy for a man or a woman to refrain from adultery, but it is not as easy to refrain from glances of the

[30]Fénelon, *Christian Perfection*, 8.
[31]de Sales, *Introduction to a Devout Life*, 212.

eyes, from giving or receiving marks of love, or from uttering or listening to flattery. . . . Wherefore I say, that being ever ready to fight courageously against great temptations, we must in the meantime diligently defend ourselves against those that seem small and inconsiderable.[32]

We would eagerly live like an ascetic for a day or two if only we could grant ourselves the privilege of then forgetting about religion and living the rest of the week with no serious claim upon our lives. Yet we have an enemy who is willing to surrender the yards lost during heroic measures in order to gain the miles won when we return to soft living.

John Climacus wrote, "Let us pay attention to another trick of our enemy. Just as bad food makes one sick after some time or indeed after some days, the same can happen in the case of actions that defile the soul. I have seen men give way to soft living and not notice at once the onset of the enemy. . . . In this they were deceived and encouraged to grow careless and to imagine that they were safe and at peace. Then came sudden destruction."[33]

One day of fasting and prayer every week cannot overcome six days of Christless living. Of course, we may not realize our lifestyles are compromised, especially if we use the world's yardstick to measure our sanctification. William Law warned, "A person that eats and drinks too much does not feel such effects from it as those do who live in notorious instances of gluttony and intemperance; but yet his course of indulgence, though it be not scandalous in the eyes of the world nor such as torments his own conscience, is a great and constant hindrance to his improvement in virtue; it gives

[32]Ibid., 301–2.
[33]Climacus, *The Ladder of Divine Ascent*, 179.

him eyes that see not and ears that hear not; it creates a sensuality in the soul, increases the power of bodily passions, and makes him incapable of entering into the true spirit of religion."[34]

This doesn't mean, however, that the antidote to small compromises is legalistic fussiness. Francis de Sales warned us that though the little temptations are dangerous, we do not serve ourselves by becoming preoccupied with them.

> As to these smaller temptations . . . as it is impossible to be altogether freed from them, the best defense that we can make is not to give ourselves much trouble about them; for although they may tease us, yet they can never hurt us, so long as we continue firmly resolved to dedicate ourselves in earnest to the service of God. . . . Content yourself with quietly removing them, not by contending or disputing with them, but by performing some actions of a contrary nature to the temptation, especially acts of the love of God. . . . This grand remedy is so terrible to the enemy of our souls, that as soon as he perceives that his temptation incites us to form acts of divine love he ceases to tempt us. . . . He who would wish to contend with them in particular would give himself much trouble to little or no purpose.[35]

This "treating the vice with the opposite virtue" is a favorite tactic of de Sales. "Consider . . . what passions are most predominant in your soul; and, having discovered them, adopt such a method of thinking, speaking, and acting, as may contradict them."[36]

Instead of praying, "Please, God, help me to never do that

[34]Law, *A Serious Call*, 191-92.
[35]de Sales, *Introduction to a Devout Life*, 303-4.
[36]Ibid., 304.

again," we can pray for the opposite: "Please, God, help me to be kinder, more patient, etc." Instead of focusing on losing a bad temper, we can focus on cultivating gentleness. Instead of trying to stop gossiping, we can focus on saying kind and encouraging things about others. Instead of focusing on ambition, we can go out of our way to serve others and help them succeed, even at our own expense.

Replacing the vice with the virtue can also be used to change our social environments. I worked in a department store to supplement a small college-pastor's salary, and the backbiting and slander there were worse than anywhere I had ever worked. After praying about the situation, I came up with a plan. When I was alone with one worker, I solicited a positive reply about another worker by asking a leading question. "Don't you think Mary is good with customers?"

The coworker answered, "Yes, I do. She really knows what she's talking about." I then waited until the next shift when I was alone with Mary. "Susan talked to me today about how helpful you are with the customers."

"Oh really?" Mary said. "Susan's a sweet gal; she's a great person to work with."

Of course, the next time I worked, Susan heard what Mary had said. I repeated the same plan with as many coworkers as possible, "gossiping positively" as much as I could. The atmosphere of our department changed because I planted a virtue, not because I gave everybody a sermon about the evil of gossip.

De Sales also urged us to use this practice before temptation strikes—thus being proactive instead of reactive. "In time of peace, that is, when temptations to the sin to which you are most inclined do not molest you, make several acts of the contrary virtue."[37] Are you always worrying? Then find things to be thankful for in times when worry is absent.

Just as failing in one area slowly eats away at our spiritual lives, so improving in one area, even a small one, nourishes our spiritual lives. Law wrote, "A man of business that has brought one part of his affairs under certain rules is in a fair way to take the same care of the rest. So he that has brought any one part of his life under the rules of religion may thence be taught to extend the same order and regularity into other parts of his life."[38]

Once we learn how to make sin our servant and then grow consistently, we must learn to avoid the trap of soul sadness.

Soul Sadness

A Pharisee who does nothing but focus on avoiding sin is still concentrating on sin, which makes him or her little different from the person who voraciously lives in sin. Both are consumed by sin—one to avoid it, the other to live in it.

Undue fretting leads to "soul sadness," or despondency or "inquietude," as Francis de Sales put it. Soul sadness is the result of a performance-based holiness and it often plagues those who most want to serve God.

De Sales wrote that true holiness is cultivated with "patience, meekness, humility, and tranquillity, expecting it more from the providence of God than from [our] own industry or diligence." If, however, we seek deliverance from sin out of performance (which is merely a form of self-love and self-exaltation), we will fatigue ourselves and fall into a soul sadness that, "instead of removing, aggravates the evil, and

[37]Ibid., 306.
[38]Law, *A Serious Call*, 111.

involves [the soul] in such anguish and distress, with so great loss of courage and strength," that we imagine ourselves "incurable."[39]

Thus de Sales asserted that soul sadness, resulting from self-love and self-effort, "is the greatest evil that can befall the soul, sin only excepted." Soul sadness saps our strength, which is needed to resist the temptation. This is how it keeps us in the maze of "performance."

It is possible for us to desire holiness for the wrong reasons; perhaps we simply want to use holiness for fame, as others might use a beautiful voice or eloquent speech. Or perhaps we are steeped in pride and simply unwilling to count ourselves among the truly sinful. This unholy desire for holiness produces a soul sadness that Satan exploits to further defeat us, with the intent of driving us off the cliff of despair.

Soul sadness "proceeds from an inordinate desire of being delivered from the evil which we feel, or of acquiring the good which we desire: and yet there is nothing which tends more to increase evil, and to prevent the enjoyment of good, than an unquiet mind."[40]

The essence of the Christian life is a love relationship with God. Our standing in the Christian life rests with Christ; when the virtues take on too much importance, that is, when acquiring virtues and avoiding sin become the primary focus of our walk, we have elevated the (admittedly important) secondary over the primary.[41] Another way of putting it is that we have made an idol out of our own piety.

[39]de Sales, *Introduction to a Devout Life*, 307.

[40]Ibid., 307–8.

[41]"When we try to pursue virtues to either extreme, vices appear and imperceptibly slip into the same paths, imperceptible at the infinitesimal end of the scale and in masses at the infinite end, so that we get lost amid the vices and can no longer see the virtues. We take issue even with perfection" (Pascal, *Pensées*, 264–65).

Holy holiness results from a tranquil reliance on God for the care of our souls. Holy holiness depends on grace, not self-effort, and it cooperates with God, rather than tries to replace God. Holy holiness recognizes that apart from God we can't help but sin, and it is willing to live with this truth, for holy holiness is simply another way of describing humble holiness.

When we want to be freed from sin, then, or to do something good for the kingdom of God, we must be careful to "settle our mind in repose and tranquillity" and *gently* seek what we desire. De Sales explained, "When I say *gently,* I do not mean negligently, but without hurry, trouble or inquietude; otherwise, instead of obtaining the effect of your desire, you will mar all, and embarrass yourself the more."[42]

De Sales wrote elsewhere, "As the mild and affectionate reproofs of a father have far greater power to reclaim his child than rage and passion; so when we have committed any fault, if we reprehend our heart with mild and calm remonstrances, having more compassion for it than passion against it, sweetly encouraging it to amendment, the repentance it shall conceive by this means will sink much deeper, and penetrate it more effectually, than a fretful, injurious, and stormy repentance."[43]

Fénelon brings this idea to a firm conclusion with the words, "Go forward always with confidence, without letting yourself be touched by the grief of a sensitive pride, which cannot bear to see itself imperfect. Your fault will serve, by this inner confusion, to make you die to yourself, to detach you from God's gifts, and to annihilate yourself to him."[44]

[42]de Sales, *Introduction to a Devout Life,* 308.
[43]Ibid., 159.
[44]Fénelon, *Christian Perfection,* 186.

The Presence in the Passion

Holy holiness is a relational holiness—it is God's over-whelming presence in my life, causing me to want to do what He wills as He gives me the strength to do it, however imperfectly I may live it out. What God wills is the dividing line of what is right and what is wrong. This may call me to die to some perfectly "legitimate" activities that, for one reason or another, God doesn't want me to participate in. Pascal urged us:

> Let us change the rule we have hitherto adopted for judging what is good. We took our own will as rule; let us now take the will of God. Anything that he wills is good and right for us, and anything he does not will is bad and wrong. . . . Other things which he left without a general prohibition, and which are therefore called permissible, are none the less not always permissible. For when God removes some particular thing from us and it becomes apparent through the event, which is evidence of God's will, that it is not his will that we should have the thing, it is then forbidden as much as sin, since it is God's will that we should not have one any more than the other. . . . While God does not will it, we must regard it as sin, as long as God's will, sole source of good and right, is against it and makes it bad and wrong.[45]

The essence of holy holiness is loving God. The more we love God, the more we will want to live according to His will. Fénelon says, "Let us plunge into [the love of God]. The more we love him, the more we love also all that which he

[45]Pascal, *Pensées*, 325. See also Law, *A Serious Call*, 316: "The whole nature of virtue consists in conforming, and the whole nature of vice in declining from the will of God"; and Fénelon, *Christian Perfection*, 76: "To want all that God wants, always to want it, for all occasions and without reservations, this is the kingdom of God which is all within."

makes us do. It is this love which consoles us in our losses, which softens our crosses for us, which detaches us from all which it is dangerous to love, which preserves us from a thousand poisons, which shows us a benevolent compassion through all the ills which we suffer, which even in death opens for us an eternal glory and happiness. It is this love which changes all our evils to good."[46]

Reflections

Quickly read 2 Samuel 11:2–17, 26–27; and 12:1–23 for background and then carefully read Psalm 51. Is David's holiness based on performance or God's grace? How does David's response to sin avoid the trap of soul sadness? Is David being harsh or gentle with himself? What could David learn from the sin? (How can he make it his servant?) What do you think was the root cause that led to David's fall? How could he have avoided it? How would you advise him to grow in the future?

[46]Fénelon, *Christian Perfection*, 41.

Chapter Five

Joyful Surrender: Christian Submission

> *What [God] asks is a will which will no longer be divided between him and any creature, a will pliant in his hands, which neither desires anything nor refuses anything, which wants without reservation everything which he wants, and which never, under any pretext, wants anything which he does not want.*   Fénelon
>
> *I should like to persuade spiritual persons that the road leading to God does not entail a multiplicity of considerations, methods, manners, and experiences . . . but demands only the one thing necessary: true self-denial, exterior and interior, through surrender of self both to suffering for Christ and to annihilation in all things.*
>
> John of the Cross

In 1654 Blaise Pascal faced his life's greatest test. His friendship with a duke had brought him into the highest levels of society, but the attractions and amusements of high society threatened his burgeoning spirituality. A letter Pascal wrote to his sister at this time reveals his inner crisis.

On the night of November 23, Pascal had an ecstatic experience that affected him for the rest of his life. In fact, he wrote down the insights he gained that night and sewed them into his jacket, transferring them from garment to garment as the jacket wore out. While he maintained some of his former relationships after the experience, he no longer felt any ambivalence about his call to surrender to God's will for his life and work.

About two years later, Pascal began making notes for what he hoped would become a full-scale apology of the Christian religion. He wanted to use the brilliant mathematical mind God had given him to defend the faith.

Pascal's notes now fill up several hundred pages in the book we know as *Pensées*. The scope of what Pascal intended must have been enormous because he stated that it would take ten years of good health to bring the book to completion—this from a man who had already accomplished more in his first thirty-five years than most people accomplish in a lifetime.

The notes were made in 1657 and 1658, but in 1659 Pascal entered a period of serious illness from which he never fully recovered. In the midst of his illness he wrote, *"Priere pour demander a Dieu le bon usage des maladies"* ("Prayer asking God for the right use of illnesses") in which he tried to find a Christian meaning for his suffering so he could discern God's will and submit to it wholly and trustfully. In the prayer, Pascal asked God to dispose of his health and his sickness, his life and his death, first for the glory of God, then for his salvation and for the good of the church.[1]

Pascal could have been bitter. He could have argued that God was treating him unfairly. He could have said, "God, I gave up everything to serve You in this, and now I'm too sick to complete it. How can You allow this to happen?" Instead

[1] Hugh Davidson, *Blaise Pascal* (Boston: Twayne Publishers, 1983), 20–21.

he again changed his direction. Because he was too ill to work hard on the apology, he devoted his final years to ministering to the poor. He didn't go back to the world; he simply found a new way to carry out his desire to serve God.

During his life, Pascal argued against the theology of the Roman Catholic Jesuits and the Protestant Calvinists, so there are, no doubt, plenty of traditions that could find fault with him, but when I read his biography I am virtually moved to tears by the heart of this man who was so surrendered to God. He surrendered not only the temptations of the world—this I can understand—but also the glory of a particular service to God—and this is what humbles me. *Everything* was placed upon the altar, and there was no bitterness at all when God decided to keep it. Pascal just kept serving the Lord.

God, make me like that man!

Surrender doesn't come easy to me. As a third-born child, by disposition and perhaps by birth-order I've grown to be somewhat of a striver. Call me to sacrifice for Jesus, and I'll quickly raise my hand. Tell me to take a risk for the Lord, and I'm willing. But ask me to surrender?

No thanks.

It has taken me some time to learn that the real test of true faith is not how successful we are, but how surrendered we are. The Christian faith is a faith in which we are called to die daily (Luke 9:23, among others). A Christian with his or her own agenda is like a horse with a head on both ends. There will be nothing but a "push-me/pull-you" struggle between this person and God. That is why Christ said the entrance to faith is through the cross; we cut off our own heads—our will—in order to follow God and His will.

The most Christian prayer we can ever pray is the prayer Jesus prayed in Gethsemane—"Lord, thy will, not mine, be done." So it should be no surprise that when Jesus taught His disciples to pray, He first blessed God, "Hallowed be Thy name," and then began with "Thy kingdom come, Thy will be done."

Christian health is not defined by how happy we are, how prosperous or healthy we are, or even by how many people we have led to the Lord in the last year. Christian health is ultimately defined by how sincerely we wave our flag of surrender.

The questions leading to spiritual growth and health, then, are: What is God's will for me in this hour and day? Where is God leading me? How can I surrender to Him?

Law provided a clue: "He therefore is the devout man who lives no longer to his own will, or the way and spirit of the world, but to the sole will of God, who considers God in everything, who serves God in everything, who makes all the parts of his common life parts of piety by doing everything in the name of God and under such rules as are conformable to His glory."[2]

We want to baptize our old nature rather than trade it in. We're not told to wash the old nature, however, but to kill it. True Christianity is a state in which we are utterly, absolutely, and completely surrendered to God.

The Two Essential Questions

My journey to surrender to God led me to two fundamental questions. The first question was: Is God good? Only if we truly believe in the goodness of God can we entrust ourselves so completely to His care.

[2]Law, *A Serious Call*, 47.

The second question was: Is God Lord? That is, does God actually and truly rule over the affairs of His world?

Both the goodness and providence of God are well established in Scripture,[3] but both are questioned today: "If God is so good, why does He allow evil things to happen?" and "If God is in control, why is the world such a mess?" Until we resolve these two questions in our own minds, we will find ourselves at virtual war with God.

I am not suggesting it is inappropriate to wrestle with the questions. They are fair questions, and we need to be honest about our inhibitions if we are ever to enter into a new intimacy with the Father. However, maturity will eventually require that we come to this conclusion: "Yes, God is good, and yes, God is Lord." Until we have done that, the intimacy of surrender simply will not be possible.

How can we ask ourselves to surrender to a God of whom we're suspicious? And even if we convince ourselves He's good, how can we surrender to Him if we think He's unaware, inactive, or powerless to make a difference?

The men and women who wrote the classics of Christian devotion believed in God's goodness and His lordship. Thomas à Kempis had this to say about the goodness of God— notice how this was the foundation for his call to surrender:

Do with me whatever it shall please thee. For it can not be anything but good, whatever thou shalt do with me. If it be thy will I should be in darkness, be thou blessed; and if it be thy will I should be in light, be thou again blessed. If thou grant me comfort, be thou blessed; and if thou wilt have me afflicted, be

[3]For Scriptures related to the goodness of God, see Genesis 50:20; Exodus 34:6-7; Psalm 25:8-10; Psalm 100:5; John 10:11; Romans 8:28; 1 Peter 2:3; and James 1:27. For those related to the providence of God, see Genesis 50:20; Job 38:41; Psalm 2:1-6; Daniel 4:34-35; Matthew 5:45; and Acts 2:23.

thou still equally blessed. My son, such as this ought to be thy state, if thou desire to walk with Me. Thou must be as ready to suffer as to rejoice. Thou must cheerfully be as destitute and poor, as full and rich.[4]

William Law wrote this about God's providence:

Every man is to consider himself as a particular object of God's providence, under the same care and protection of God as if the world had been made for him alone. It is not by chance that any man is born at such a time, of such parents, and in such place and condition. . . . Every soul comes into the body at such a time and in such circumstances by the express designment of God, according to some purposes of His will and for some particular ends.[5]

We will find it impossible to move forward in surrender if we do not find ourselves agreeing with Thomas à Kempis regarding God's goodness and William Law regarding God's providence. Many of us carry wounds that need to be healed before we can embrace these two truths. Since surrender is fundamental to the Christian faith, we need to do the soul work that is necessary to arrive at an understanding of God's goodness and God's providence. Others of us may have some intellectual mountains to climb before we can wave our white flags of surrender. Whatever the case, we should do what we must do so we can resolve these two fundamental questions without delay.

The scrapper in each of us must be retired.

[4]à Kempis, *The Imitation of Christ*, III:17:1-2.
[5]Law, *A Serious Call*, 322.

The Surrendered Heart

Testimony to the surrendered heart is the hallmark of a Christian classic. It is not a coincidence that so many of the ancients have written about it. Consider just these examples:

Ignatius Loyola: "We do not for our part wish for health rather than sickness, for wealth rather than poverty, for honor rather than dishonor, for a long life rather than a short one; and so in all other things, desiring and choosing only those which most lead us to the end for which we were created."[6]

Thomas à Kempis: "Lord how often shall I resign myself, and wherein shall I forsake myself? Always, and every hour; as well in small things as in great. I except nothing, but do desire that thou be found divested of all things. Otherwise how canst thou be mine, and I thine, unless thou be stripped of all self-will, both within and without?"[7]

Teresa of Avila: "The whole aim of any person who is beginning prayer—and don't forget this, because it's very important—should be that he work and prepare himself with determination and every possible effort to bring his will into conformity with God's will. . . . It is the person who lives in more perfect conformity who will receive more from the Lord and be more advanced on this road."[8]

And my favorite, by John of the Cross: "I should like to persuade spiritual persons that the road leading to God does not entail a multiplicity of considerations, methods, manners, and experiences—though in their own way these may be a requirement for beginners—but demands only the one thing

[6]Ignatius Loyola, *The Text of the Spiritual Exercises of Saint Ignatius*, (Westminster, Md.: The Newman Bookshop, 1943), 34.

[7]à Kempis, *The Imitation of Christ*, III:37:1.

[8]Teresa of Avila, *The Interior Castle*, II:1:8.

necessary: true self-denial, exterior and interior, through surrender of self both to suffering for Christ and to annihilation in all things. . . . If one fails in this exercise, the root and sum total of all the virtues, the other methods would amount to no more than going about in circles without any progress, even if they result in considerations and communications as lofty as those of the angels."[9]

I quote all of these saints in length to purposefully overwhelm you with the surrendered heart of those who have already walked the Christian journey. They went far in the Christian life because they surrendered to God and resolved to cooperate with Him rather than fight and question Him throughout their entire lives.

There will likely be a time in our Christian journeys when, like Jacob, we will wrestle with God all night long. That night may last for months or even years. But there must eventually come a dawn when we say, "OK, God, You win. You've broken me and I'm Yours. No more fighting. No more complaining. Lead me where You will. Not my will but Thine be done."

The Biggest Block

The biggest block to our surrender is not our appetites and wayward desires, but our addiction to running our own lives. Surrender would be easy if it allowed us to merely sacrifice a few leaves, a few choice sins. But God wants more. God's ax hits the trunk.

Pascal, who knew the heartrending call of surrender, wrote, "True conversion consists in self-annihilation before the universal being whom we have so often vexed and who is

[9]John of the Cross, "The Ascent of Mount Carmel," in *John of the Cross: Selected Writings*, ed. and trans. by Kieran Kavanaugh (New York: Paulist Press, 1987), II:7:8.

perfectly entitled to destroy us at any moment, in recognizing that we can do nothing without him and that we have deserved nothing but his disfavor."[10]

The failure to truly die to ourselves is devastating to our spiritual health. Thomas à Kempis said, "the love of thyself doth hurt thee more than anything in the world."[11] This is because without the resignation of self, we will be involved in petty turf wars every time God tries to break in. Do you ever find yourself bargaining with God? I do. "God, I'll do this if You'll do that." When I read Thomas à Kempis, however, I realized there can be no conditions to our true surrender. God is Lord of the universe—He is not a used-car salesman. Here are the words that challenged me:

> Some there are who resign themselves, but with certain exceptions: for they put not their whole trust in God, therefore, they study how to provide for themselves. Some also at first offer all, but afterward being assailed with temptation, they return again to their own place, and therefore they make no progress in the path of virtue. These shall not attain to the true liberty of a pure heart, nor to the grace of my sweetest familiarity, unless they first make an entire resignation and a daily sacrifice of themselves unto me. For without this, there neither is nor can be a fruitful union with me.[12]

An equally difficult lesson for me to learn was that surrender is never a once-in-a-lifetime activity; it is the continual worship of a growing Christian. This means that I must be willing to part with anything on a regular basis, even those

[10]Pascal, *Pensées*, 137.
[11]à Kempis, *The Imitation of Christ*, III:27:1.
[12]Ibid., III:37:2.

good things that come from God. As part of our discipline of surrender, God will often ask us to let go of something very precious, even something He has given us. This is because, as Fénelon wrote, "There is not a single gift, noble as it may be, which, after having been a means of advancement, does not generally become, later on, a trap and an obstacle, by the return of self which soils the soul. For this reason God takes away what he has given. But he does not take it away to deprive us of it for ever. He takes it away so that he can better give it, so that he can give it back without the impurity of this evil sense of ownership which we mingle with it without noticing it in ourselves. The loss of the gift takes away our ownership. . . . Then the gift is no longer the gift of God. It is God himself in the soul. It is no more a gift of God, because we consider it no longer as something apart from him, and something which the soul can possess."[13]

Just months before my wife and I became engaged, Lisa was in Mexico on a short-term missions trip. She sent me a letter explaining that she was considering staying in Mexico for another year. A close friend, sensing my anxiety over Lisa's plans, wrote me a letter after he had spent some time praying for us. Rob said I had to hold Lisa like I held sand— with an open palm. If I closed my fist too tightly, the sand would run through my fingers.

I knew Rob had heard God correctly, but his words were the last words I wanted to hear. As I said before, surrender has never been easy for me; but this time, I let go. Lisa ended up coming back, and we were engaged just a couple months later.

How many Christians have wondered why a precious rela-

[13]Fénelon, *Christian Perfection*, 171–72.

tionship has seemed to go sour, a powerful ministry appears to be drying up, or a healthy business seems to be disintegrating? Could it be that we have taken what is good and begun worshiping the created rather than the Creator? It would be simplistic to suggest this is always the case but presumptuous to assume it is never the case. God blesses us, and we become so enamored with the blessing that we lose sight of the One who blesses.

Surrender is thus the daily worship of a true Christian—and not just in the big things either. If we gladly relinquish the "small little sacrifices," our growth will be great, for any small surrender is a great victory; any refusal of surrender is a great defeat.

We need to understand the seriousness of rebellion. When we refuse God in the big things, He will move to the small. When we refuse to give God even these, what else can He ask? We have then approached the land of apostasy, and all the spiritual disciplines in the world, all the beautiful songs we sing, and all the money we give away won't excuse the fact that our hearts are in rebellion.

Christian surrender means the death of complaining.

The Death of Complaining

If we truly believe in God's goodness and His lordship, there is no reason to complain. William Law pointed out that "resignation to the divine will signifies a cheerful approbation and thankful acceptance of everything that comes from God. It is not enough patiently to submit, but we must thankfully receive and fully approve of everything that by the order of God's providence happens to us. . . .

"It is very common for people to allow themselves great

liberty in finding fault with such things as have only God for their cause. . . . It sounds indeed much better to murmur at the course of the world or the state of things than to murmur at providence, to complain of the seasons and weather, than to complain of God, but if these have no other cause but God and His providence it is a poor distinction to say that you are only angry at the things but not at the cause and director of them."[14]

It will be hard for many of us to admit we are complaining about God, but honesty is essential if we are to be delivered from this sin. We can't gripe about every decision a coach or a politician makes and then pretend we support him or her. At a particularly frustrating time in my life, when it felt as if God had kept me in a hole for eight long years, I found myself going through the motions of worship but continually asking, "God, why are You doing this to me?" The problem with this is that we can't worship someone we don't trust. I couldn't learn my lesson until I was broken enough to surrender, for my questioning came very close to crossing the line separating honest pain from prideful blasphemy.

I learned that faith isn't tested by how often God answers my prayers with a yes, but by my willingness to continue serving Him and *thanking* Him, even when I don't have a clue as to what He is doing. This required a radical shift in my thinking; I had to become convinced of God's oversight in my life.

When we complain, what we are really saying is, "I could have done a better job than God in this instance. If I had made the choice, I would have done this and so . . ." This is blasphemy.

[14]Law, *A Serious Call*, 317, 319.

When I looked back on the difficulty of those eight long years, I saw their necessity in a new light.

> Had you been anything else than what you are, you had, all things considered, been less wisely provided for than you are now; you had wanted some circumstances and conditions that are best fitted to make you happy yourself and serviceable to the glory of God.
>
> Could you see all that which God sees, all that happy chain of causes and motives which are to move and invite you to a right course of life, you would see something to make you like that state you are in as fitter for you than any other.
>
> But as you cannot see this, so it is here that your Christian faith and trust in God is to exercise itself and render you as grateful and thankful for the happiness of your state as if you saw everything that contributes to it with your own eyes.[15]

So there was no more room for me to complain. I found that the most potent weapon against complaining or even questioning is the gift of thanksgiving. Thanksgiving became my doorway to a more mature surrender.

Thanksgiving: The Doorway to Surrender

When I began to fight my sin of complaining with thanksgiving, the opposing virtue, this was a struggle for me. But God in His mercy placed gratitude in my heart, and like a snowball rolling down a hill, that gift of gratitude grew until the complaining was wiped out.

I then reached a crossroad where I was able to thank God even for the eight-year desert. I saw that I had so much inner

[15]Ibid., 324.

sin in me then that there was no other way for me to be healed. If God had answered my prayers for an earlier reprieve, He wouldn't have been acting out of love; He would have left me in immaturity, and I would have continued to make a mess out of my life. Law wrote:

> For if [a Christian] cannot thank and praise God as well in calamities and sufferings as in prosperity and happiness, he is as far from the piety of a Christian as he that only loves them that love him is from the charity of a Christian. For to thank God only for such things as you like is no more a proper act of piety than to believe only what you see is an act of faith.
>
> Resignation and thanksgiving to God are only acts of piety when they are acts of faith, trust, and confidence in the divine goodness.[16]

My only hope of salvation was if God could pull me away from the steering wheel of my life. The difficult period I endured was God's way of doing that, and as I realized the effectiveness of it I became thankful for it. This is when I learned that thanksgiving is a discipline, and like all the disciplines, it requires practice.

Law taught me to begin by practicing thanksgiving in the small things.

> Don't . . . please yourself with thinking how piously you would act and submit to God in a plague, a famine, or persecution, but be intent upon the perfection of the present day, and be assured that the best way of showing a true zeal is to make little things the occasions of great piety.
>
> Begin, therefore, in the smallest matters and most ordinary occasions, and accustom your mind to the daily exercise of this

[16]Ibid., 321.

pious temper in the lowest occurrences of life. And when a contempt, an affront, a little injury, loss, or disappointment, or the smallest events of every day continually raise your mind to God in proper acts of resignation, then you may justly hope that you shall be numbered amongst those that are resigned and thankful to God in the greatest trials and afflictions.[17]

Prayers of thanksgiving can be mixed with prayers of surrender for even greater effect. Thomas à Kempis provided us with a great model: "My son, say thou thus in everything: 'Lord, if this be pleasing unto thee, let it be so. Lord, if it be to thy honor, in thy name let this be done. Lord, if thou seest it good, and allowest it to be profitable for me, then grant unto me that I may use this to thine honor. But if thou knowest it will be harmful unto me, and no profit to the health of my soul, take away any such desire from me."[18]

Conformed to His Image

If our hearts are going to truly surrender to God, we must be willing to allow God to define good and evil and shape us according to His will. We must be willing, not only to do what is right, but to let God define what is right. Good is whatever God desires; evil is whatever God prohibits.

At first, conforming may simply be an act of the will. We may obey God, not necessarily because we want to, but because we know we should. However, if we are faithful in surrendering our will to God, over time we will soon begin wanting to obey. Law said, "When you love that which God loves, you act with Him, you join yourself to Him, and when

[17]Ibid., 327.
[18]à Kempis, *The Imitation of Christ*, III:15:1.

you love what He dislikes, then you oppose Him and separate yourself from Him."[19]

This is why it is so spiritually debilitating to ever willfully rebel against God. Obedience and disobedience are both habitual. Our appetites and passions are like our tastebuds—we crave what we grow used to. To experience true surrender, we must die to our own desires so God can give us new desires.

When God birthed thanksgiving in my heart, my purest cry was simply, "God, I want to be on Your side." My only request was to be wherever God was. If God was in riches or poverty, sickness or health, at home or far away, I wanted to be there. Whatever God was doing, that's what I wanted to be doing. Nothing else mattered.

The Joy and Peace of Surrender

At its root, however, surrender becomes not so much a discipline as a cry of the heart. It is a joy, and it brings great peace. Fénelon wrote, "O bridegroom of souls, thou lettest the souls which do not resist thee experience in this life an advance taste of that felicity."[20]

This "taste of felicity," however, is dependent upon true surrender. Fénelon told us our hearts, not just our wills, must be changed. "If we are . . . faithful in breaking internally with creatures, that is, in stopping them from entering the depths of our hearts, which our Lord has kept to dwell in and to be respected, worshipped and loved in, we shall soon taste the pure joy which God will not fail to give to a soul which is free and detached from all human affection."[21]

[19]Law, *A Serious Call*, 256.
[20]Fénelon, *Christian Perfection*, 168.
[21]Ibid., 28.

The glory of the Christian life is found in the fact that God doesn't ask us to surrender to just difficult things. At first it may seem like that, but eventually, if we don't hold back, we'll find that God's will is for us to surrender to many very wonderful things. Again, it all comes back to trusting in His goodness. When we surrender to a good God, we shouldn't be surprised that we must surrender to good things. Sin tastes sweet but turns bitter in our stomachs. Holiness often tastes bitter but turns sweet in our stomachs.

These little ecstasies are merely tastes of what awaits us in heaven. It would be dangerous for God to give them to us without limit, so He places boundaries on what we can experience. "Consolation shall be sometimes given thee, but the abundant fullness thereof shall not be granted," wrote Thomas à Kempis.[22] But even these consolations will be worth far more to us than the trinkets provided by the world, and that is the true blessing of surrender. Because God is good, He calls us to surrender to good things.

One of the joys of surrender is a deep peace. Rebellion means war, so it is no surprise that surrender means peace. This peace gives us a new freedom in our relationships. As always, true Christian spirituality has implications for community living in families and churches. Thomas à Kempis said if we are not surrendered to God, we will be at war with others. "He that is well in peace, is not suspicious of any man. But he that is discontented and troubled, is tossed with divers suspicions: he is neither at rest himself nor suffereth others to be at rest. . . . He considereth what others are bound to do, and neglecteth that which he is bound to himself."[23]

[22]à Kempis, *The Imitation of Christ*, III:49:4.
[23]Ibid., II:3:1.

I suspect that a thousand years from now I'll have a pretty good understanding of why my life has gone the way it has; for now, I'm content to trust that God knows what He is doing.

Our model in this is Christ, à Kempis wrote. He imagined Christ saying, "Of My own will did I offer up Myself unto God the Father for thy sins, My hands being stretched forth on the cross, and My body laid bare, so that nothing remained in Me that was not wholly turned into a sacrifice for the appeasing of the divine Majesty. In like manner oughtest thou also to offer thyself willingly unto Me every day . . . with all thy strength and affections, and to the utmost stretch of thine inward faculties. What do I require of thee more, than that thou study to resign thyself entirely unto Me?"[24]

God will not lay down His arms. He has declared war on all who stand in rebellion. The vanquished receive eternal life; the obstinate are condemned by their own foolishness. But there will be no peace until we surrender. Surrender to God is the essence—and the greatest blessing—of the Christian life.

Reflections

Copy the following prayer, written by Francis de Sales:

And, turning myself towards my most gracious and merciful God, I desire, purpose, and am irrevocably resolved to serve and love him now and forever; and to this end, I give and consecrate to him my soul with all its powers, my heart with all its affections, and my body with all its senses, protesting that I will never more abuse any part of my being against his divine will and sovereign

[24]Ibid., IV:8:1.

majesty, to whom I offer up and sacrifice myself in spirit, to be forever his loyal, obedient, and faithful creature, without ever revoking or repenting of this my act and deed.

But if, alas! I should chance, through the suggestion of the enemy, or through human frailty, to transgress in any point, or fail in adhering to this my resolution and dedication, I protest from this moment, and am determined, with the assistance of the Holy Ghost, to rise as soon as I shall perceive my fall, and return again to the divine mercy, without any delay whatsoever. This is my inviolable and irrevocable will, intention, and resolution, which I declare and confirm without reservation or exception, in the sacred presence of God.[25]

If you can, in good conscience, sign the paper on which you've copied this prayer, claiming it as the prayer of your heart, do so and mark the date. Then carry this prayer with you. When God's Spirit prompts your heart to surrender and you feel yourself resisting, take the prayer out of your purse or wallet and read it, reminding yourself of the pledge you have made by the grace of God.

[25]de Sales, *Introduction to a Devout Life*, 51–52.

Chapter Six

Cultivating the Quiet: Simplicity

For that is the cause why there are so few contemplative persons to be found, for that few can wholly withdraw themselves from things created and perishing.

Thomas à Kempis

The sole cause of man's unhappiness is that he does not know how to stay quietly in his room. Blaise Pascal

[To practice the presence of God] the heart must be empty of all else, because God wills to possess the heart alone; and as He cannot possess it alone unless it be empty of all besides, so He cannot work in it what He would, unless it be left vacant to Him. Brother Lawrence

---

It can happen so suddenly.

I was traveling alone and thus had plenty of free time to reflect without distraction. The airport was bustling, but all of the activity around me seemed slow compared with the racing thoughts in my mind. It had been a busy week; I had hardly thought about the two speaking engagements ahead of me until now, just as I was about to get on the plane.

Although my thoughts were bouncing around in a very

undisciplined manner, they kept landing on finances. I was trying to figure out how we could squeeze some extra money out of the budget for Christmas. I had been reading several books on personal finances, two on how to live more simply, and one on sound investing.

I had told the organizers of the first group I was speaking to, "Forget about any honorarium," but I have to confess that I was now thinking the honorarium could have helped to solve my problem.

Then God's voice cut in. In the busyness of the airport, God quieted my heart. He showed me how I was ostensibly traveling to bring His Word to others, but I was consumed with money. He showed me how money had become a motivator in my life—even worse, a motivator that was competing with my heart's desire to share God's Word.

I couldn't make a defense. I was guilty. I had let concerns become worries, which then became preoccupations, which then became sins. Money wasn't the primary issue; it was just the latest worry stealing my heart. My main problem was that I had let my heart become too full to hear God in the quiet.

That's when I realized that simplicity is a journey. We can make significant gains toward living a simple life only to find ourselves falling back. Money is just one of the many temptations that make simplicity so hard to achieve, so I want to make one thing very clear: When we mention simplicity in this chapter, we are not talking about sewing gunny sacks into clothes; in fact, after this we will hardly mention money at all. The ancients held that simplicity starts in the heart. Simplicity is a freedom from worries and concerns about all things, not just finances. It is thus the doorway to a deeper and richer walk with God, which is often blocked by our active game of hide-and-seek.

Our Game of Hide-and-Seek

The sin many of us fall into is not that we shake our fists at God and defy Him to His face; that is the sin of unbelievers. Our sin is that we passively rebel against God, filling our lives with so much noise and busyness that God's voice cannot, or will not, penetrate.

Fénelon wrote, "God does not cease speaking, but the noise of the creatures without, and of our passions within, deafens us, and stops our hearing. We must silence every creature, we must silence ourselves, to hear in the deep hush of the whole soul, the ineffable voice of the spouse. We must bend the ear, because it is a gentle and delicate voice, only heard by those who no longer hear anything else."[1]

Cultivating the quiet is a painful experience when we are addicted to noise, excitement, and occupation. Opening the door to spiritual quiet can also open the door to spiritual fear and loneliness. It takes a great amount of courage to face God.

According to Pascal, we're often afraid that if we start to slow down, the truth of our deeply felt misery will assail us. We lack the courage to confront this misery, so we force ourselves to live at breakneck speed with maximum noise so we will be too numb or too busy to notice the pain.

Pascal believed that many young people live in a fundamen-

[1]Fénelon, *Christian Perfection,* 155–56.

tally dishonest existence, pretending they're having a good time while they live in constant terror of the truth of their hearts. Their "lives are all noise, diversions, and thoughts for the future. But take away their diversion and you will see them bored to extinction. Then they feel their nullity without recognizing it, for nothing could be more wretched than to be intolerably depressed as soon as one is reduced to introspection with no means of diversion."[2]

Augustine wrote that although adults frequently attack this youthful addiction to diversions, they are often guilty of doing the same thing. He admitted that, as a young man, his "sole delight was play; and for this [he was] punished by those who yet themselves were doing the like. But elder folks' idleness is called 'business'; that of boys, being really the same, is punished by those elders."[3]

Pascal agreed with Augustine, writing that even a king without diversion is a very wretched man.[4] Young or old, rich or poor, it doesn't matter—the thing we fear most is quiet; therefore what we lack is peace, making us very unhappy people. Our lust for diversion proves our unhappiness, for if we were truly happy, Pascal noted, "we should not need to divert ourselves from thinking about it."[5]

Our chaos of the soul and busyness of the spirit robs us of our created destiny to find fulfillment in a relationship with God. A voice deep within our souls tells us something is wrong, but we are too afraid to slow down and find out how life could be different. Pascal explained:

[2]Pascal, *Pensées*, 38.
[3]Augustine, *Confessions*, I:15.
[4]Pascal, *Pensées*, 71–72.
[5]Ibid., 48.

They have a secret instinct driving them to seek external diversion and occupation, and this is the result of their constant sense of wretchedness. They have another secret instinct, left over from the greatness of our original nature, telling them that the only true happiness lies in rest and not in excitement. These two contrary instincts give rise to a confused plan buried out of sight in the depths of their soul, which leads them to seek rest by way of activity and always to imagine that the satisfaction they miss will come to them once they overcome certain obvious difficulties and cap open the door to welcome rest. All our life passes in this way: we seek rest by struggling against certain obstacles, and once they are overcome, rest proves intolerable because of the boredom it produces. We must get away from it and crave excitement.[6]

Pascal said the boredom that drives us to diversion could be the catalyst that calls us to change—if only we were not afraid to do the necessary work. But Satan offers us his narcotics as alternatives, and they bring us "imperceptibly to our death." Much of our television watching is a quiet, sleepless death in which we kill our souls by letting time race by. We can spend several hours in front of the television, and what have we gained? We haven't talked to anyone, we haven't accomplished anything, and we usually haven't gained any insight or inspiration. Yet time has slipped by, and it will never return again. In essence, we have willingly forfeited a precious slice of the time God has given us on this earth.

The difficulty of simplicity is that it will, at times (especially in the early stages as we break our addiction to diversion),

[6]Ibid., 69.

lead us into soul boredom, gloom, depression, and possibly even to despair. These are facts of the spiritual life that have to be confronted. I would be less than honest if I suggested that one day our lives are filled with diversions and the next day we walk hand-in-hand with God in glorious rapture. A drug addict cannot expect to give up drugs without paying the price of withdrawal. We who have been drugged by diversions cannot expect to enter the quiet without a struggle. Our souls will roar for diversion, the fix that saves us from God's presence.

It takes great courage to confront these demons of boredom and fear. They need merely to show their faces and we tend to dutifully lapse into unceasing activity to escape them. But we *must* escape them. If we allow fear and boredom to push us back into these diversions, we will never know the blessing of simplicity. We must push through fear and boredom if we are to seek the face of God.

God is more than a revealer; He is also the healer. Our sadness and our misery can be transformed, but not by running from them. God calls us into the quiet (Isa. 30:15), not to chastise us, but to draw us into a deeper communion with Him. If we are to quit hiding from God, we need to know why we hide.

The Reasons We Hide from God

When we get too close to God, the supernatural agitation in our hearts reminds us that we are dealing with Aslan, the fierce and regal lion who, as Lucy found out in C. S. Lewis's Chronicles of Narnia, is anything but a tamed lion. We cannot control God; and what we can't control, we often fear and therefore avoid.

Yes, it will take great courage to enter the quiet and dismember our distractions. We are spiritually fearful people, and alone before God, we stand naked and vulnerable. We won't be able to pretend anymore; before God, we will have the choice to obey or to disobey, but pretending will no longer be an option. If we are miserable, we will have to face our misery. If we are sad, we will have to face our sadness. When we dwell in God's presence, we must dwell in truth; we cannot control the outcome.

Others of us may hide because we fear the test of faith. We suspect that when we get down on our knees, instead of being met by an overwhelming sense of God's presence we'll face a seemingly eternal void, a loud nothingness that chills our faith and tempts us to doubt. We don't want our faith to be proven false, so we never prove it at all.

Still others of us may be unconvinced that God is able to satisfy the hunger in our souls, so we never give Him the chance. We might believe in the gospel intellectually, but we're unwilling to bet our emotional fulfillment on it.

A final reason we hide from God is that we may be living in disobedience. We may, like Jonah, be running from a duty that we know God wants us to carry out. Or we may, like Adam and Eve, be hiding because we've committed a sin and fear God's presence. We'd be happy to follow God as long as He allowed us to nurse that grudge, hold on to that inappropriate relationship, or continue in that questionable business practice.

It takes great courage to confront these tests, sometimes more courage than we possess; so rather than face them we pretend they're not tests at all, and we simply avoid God. Just as someone who is allergic to cats learns the beginning symptoms of a reaction and makes haste to get away, so we often unknowingly begin to learn the sensation of God breaking into our hearts, and we rush into some activity or diversion to avoid His presence.

Entering the Quiet

The ancients give us four themes that are particularly helpful for Christians who want to enter the quiet. They are the disciplines of a captivated heart, a bridled tongue, a limited curiosity, and a slow reentry into daily life after a time of prayer.

A Captivated Heart

Just as we have a limit to our physical strength, so we have a limit to our emotional and spiritual strength. John of the Cross said, "The more people rejoice over something outside God, the less intense will be their joy in God; and the more their hope goes out toward something else, the less there is for God."[7]

A basketball player who shows up tired for a game because he ran a marathon in the morning would get a justified and stern rebuke from his coach. A woman who showed up at work exhausted because she had been watching television all night wouldn't have an excuse for her boss. Coaches and bosses expect us to conserve our energy for what really matters.

God expects no less.

There was a defining moment in my spiritual life. It happened when I realized that if I insisted on becoming consumed by every major sporting event or political race, every move

[7]John of the Cross, "The Ascent of Mount Carmel," in *Selected Writings*, III:16:2.

of the stock market, or even every worry of parenting, if I let these things seize my heart, I simply could not enter into a true celebration of the Sabbath or the joy of a baptism, or the Lord's Supper, or Christmas and Easter, or any other true and significant celebration. I have learned the necessity of "guarding my heart" (Prov. 4:23) because my heart does not have an infinite capacity to rejoice or be alarmed. By becoming preoccupied with passing things, I exhaust my heart's ability to care about the things that really do matter. I become like the young Augustine, who said, "Thus with the baggage of this present world was I held down pleasantly, as in sleep."[8]

The deeper Christian life consists of finding ways to bring the remembrance of God into our daily existence. Fénelon urged:

> Let us become accustomed to recollect ourselves, during the day and in the course of our duties, by a single look toward God. Let us thus quiet all the movements of our hearts, as soon as we see them agitated. Let us separate ourselves from all pleasure which does not come from God. Let us cut off futile thoughts and dreams. Let us not speak empty words. Let us seek God . . . and we shall find him without fail.[9]

This "God focus" is absolutely essential to keep simplicity from becoming a prison. Fénelon says, "A continual effort to push away the thoughts, which occupy us with ourselves and our own interests, would be in itself a continual occupation with ourselves, which would distract us from the presence of God and the tasks which he wants us to accomplish. The

---

[8]Augustine, *Confessions*, VIII:11.
[9]Fénelon, *Christian Perfection*, 28–29.

important thing is sincerely to have surrendered into the hands of God all our interests in pleasure, convenience and reputation."[10]

I want to have a simple and quiet heart because I want to hear from God; I want to be captivated by Him, so I am willing to give up everything else if only I can know Him. Some of what I give up may be given back, but I will accept back only those elements that allow my God-focus to remain.

A Bridled Tongue

One of the most practical ways to enter into the quiet is to *be* quiet. A wagging tongue is proof of an overly busy mind. Ignatius wrote, "Idle words are not to be spoken, by which I mean whatever does not profit me or any one else, or whatever is not ordained to the end."[11]

John Climacus saw talkativeness as virtually the antithesis of spiritual depth and maturity. "Talkativeness is the throne of vainglory on which it loves to preen itself and show off. Talkativeness is a sign of ignorance, a doorway to slander, a leader of jesting, a servant of lies, the ruin of compunction, a summoner of despondency, a messenger of sleep, a dissipation of recollection, the end of vigilance, the cooling of zeal, the darkening of prayer. Intelligent silence is the mother of prayer, freedom from bondage, custodian of zeal, a guard on our thoughts."[12]

Climacus urged monks, "Once outside your cell, watch your tongue, for the fruits of many labors can be scattered in a moment."[13] When we are burning with the desire to speak,

[10]Ibid., 199.
[11]Ignatius Loyola, *Spiritual Exercises*, 17.
[12]Climacus, *The Ladder of Divine Ascent*, 158.
[13]Ibid., 273.

we should pause and check the source of that fire. "A man should know that a devil's sickness is on him if he is seized by the urge in conversation to assert his opinion, however correct it may be."[14]

It is ironic that those who talk the most often pray the least, frequently giving the excuse that they simply have no time. To these persons, Thomas à Kempis counseled, "If thou wilt withdraw thyself from speaking vainly, and from gadding idly, as also from listening to novelties and rumors, thou shalt find leisure enough and suitable for meditation on good things."[15]

The mark of a spiritual man or woman is a listening heart, not a lecturing tongue.[16] A simple Christian wants to hear from God; this person has little enjoyment hearing his or her own voice. As Thomas à Kempis hinted when he wrote, "withdraw thyself . . . from listening to novelties and rumors," simplicity also calls us to let go of unhealthy curiosity.

A Limited Curiosity

Simplicity frees us from being tabloid Christians. Whenever we smell a scandal, local or national, we usually want all the messy details. In this we're spiritual Peeping Toms. We may try to cover our curiosity with prayerful concern or feigned love, but often we just want to satisfy our own spiritual lusts.

Thomas à Kempis wrote, "How can he abide long in peace, who thrusts himself into the cares of others, who seeks occasions abroad, who little or seldom concentrates his own

[14]Ibid., 106.

[15]à Kempis, *The Imitation of Christ*, I:20:1.

[16]"In the multitude of words sin is not lacking, / But he who restrains his lips is wise" (Prov. 10:19 NKJV).

thoughts? Blessed are the single-hearted: for they shall enjoy much peace."[17]

We have to realize we don't need to know all that we want to know; we need to cultivate the discipline of letting go of cares that don't concern us. Thomas à Kempis warned, "My son, be not curious, nor trouble thyself with idle cares."[18] We need to trust God and those He has placed in leadership. If someone is not accountable to us, we don't need to know the details. Our responsibility is not to figure out everything but to keep ourselves at peace.

I've found that if I really want to change the world and reform the church, the best place to start is with myself. Thomas à Kempis agreed. "In every matter attend to thyself, what thou doest, and what thou sayest; and direct thy whole attention unto this, that thou mayest please me alone, and neither desire nor seek anything beside me. But as for the words or deeds of others judge nothing rashly; neither do thou entangle thyself with things not committed unto thee; and doing thus thou mayest be little or seldom disturbed."[19]

Curiosity kills our souls. It leads us to listen to gossip and then to pass that gossip on. Pascal warned, "We usually only want to know something so that we can talk about it."[20] When we dive unnecessarily and uninvited into the lives of others, we lose our own inner grounding. "Stay away from what does not concern you," Climacus urged, "for curiosity can defile stillness as nothing else can."[21]

We don't need to be judge, prosecuting attorney, and

[17]à Kempis, *The Imitation of Christ,* I:11:1.
[18]Ibid., III:24:1.
[19]Ibid., III:25:1.
[20]Pascal, *Pensées,* 50.
[21]Climacus, *The Ladder of Divine Ascent,* 273.

jury for everything that is going on around us. Our instant-information age pounds us with up-to-the-second details about many things we simply don't need to know. These incessant bulletins can weigh us down and root our thinking in transitory matters. While I was writing this book, one of the concerns everybody was talking about was the North American Free Trade Agreement (NAFTA). When a friend asked me for my opinion I surprised him by answering, "I don't have one." That quick admission allowed us to move on to a delightful conversation concerning the state of the clergy in America.

Now, admittedly, we do need to be involved in some issues, and those issues may differ from person to person. But as you read this, how important is NAFTA to you now? Do you even think about it? How did the media's treating it as their "obsession of the week" benefit you or me?

I was fascinated when I read a biography about George Washington and learned how many major events took place during the American Revolution and during Washington's first years as president that Washington didn't hear about for days after they happened. Yet was he any less effective as a leader? No, because he was guided by general principles that didn't change.

I've learned a lot from reading military history, and one of those principles applies here. In Vietnam, the infantry would form groups of circles that prevented each group of soldiers from being overrun, flanked, or ambushed by the enemy. An individual soldier's job was to protect his portion of the circle; if everyone focused on his specific task, everyone was protected. If someone wandered off, the circle would be broken and disaster would erupt.

Likewise, we each have a circle to tend. James Dobson's

circle is a lot bigger than mine. A missionary to Jordan or the head of a denomination or a stay-at-home mom will all have their own circles and they will be quite different from mine. The key is for us to recognize the boundaries of our circles and cut off undue curiosity outside of them. This doesn't mean we work *less*; it simply means we concentrate our effort on the sphere of influence God has given us and we trust Him, as our general, to fill in any gaps that open up.

I can't afford to respond to every appeal for money that crosses my desk or every desire that crosses my heart. But my mind is no less valuable and every bit as finite as my wallet, so I'm going to conserve my thoughts no less than my dollars. I refuse to let some news editor in New York dictate my topics of conversation on a day-to-day basis. Instead, I want to hear from God what He's teaching His people. I want my thoughts to be governed by eternal principles, not the latest opinion poll that nobody will care about six months from now.

Thomas à Kempis still blesses me with his words, "My son, in many things it is thy duty to be ignorant, and to esteem thyself as dead upon earth, and as one to whom the whole world is crucified. It is thy duty also to pass by many things with a deaf ear, and rather to think of those which belong unto thy peace. It is more useful to turn away one's eyes from unpleasant things, and to leave every one to his own opinion, than to be a slave to contentious discourses."[22]

A captivated heart, a bridled tongue, a limited curiosity, and a slow reentry after prayer are necessary disciplines of simplicity.

[22]à Kempis, *The Imitation of Christ*, III:44:1.

A Slow Reentry After Prayer

The goal of simplicity is communion with God, what Thomas à Kempis referred to as "spiritual contemplation." Since spiritual contemplation is largely a lost art in today's busy culture, we need to be reminded that spiritual truths, when first birthed, are fragile. A busy mind will choke them out as surely as weeds choke flowers. Francis de Sales wrote, "After prayer, be careful not to agitate your heart, lest you spill the precious balm it has received. My meaning is, that you must, for some time, if possible, remain in silence, and gently remove your heart from prayer to your other employments; retaining, as long as you can, a feeling of the affections which you have conceived."[23]

We have talked a great deal about the tyranny of the television set, but we also need to mention the tyranny of the telephone. When I am talking to God, why should I let a fifty-dollar machine break my thoughts? Who has more to reveal to me than the Creator of the universe? Rarely are telephone calls so urgent that they can't be put off for thirty minutes or so, but our inner spirit acts like it's a felony to let a telephone ring.

When we charge from prayer into the blare of diversion, we crush the small blossom God has given us for the day. The precious truths, entrusted to us by God Himself, are carelessly discarded and soon resemble dirty roses lying crushed in the middle of the street.

Rise slowly, with reverence, and keep your eye trained on God's face. This is where I find a spiritual journal so helpful. Profound insights can have a shorter shelf life than milk if I don't write them down, a practice that further implants them

[23]de Sales, *Introduction to a Devout Life*, 75.

in my mind. I view these thoughts as some of my most precious possessions, entrusted to me by God, for which I will be held accountable.

There will be occasions when we must focus on and perhaps even be largely consumed with external cares. But we don't have to remain diverted. When necessary interruptions break in, we should strive to return as quickly as we can. God is always there, waiting for us to practice His presence. Francis de Sales wrote, "Remember . . . to retire occasionally into the solitude of your heart while you are outwardly engaged in business or conversation. . . . Withdraw, then, your thoughts, from time to time, into your heart, where, separated from all men, you may familiarly treat with God on the affairs of your soul."[24]

Some of my best times of prayer occur in large crowds or at festive social gatherings. It's as if the noise and the chatter make me hunger to hear God's voice. Like a husband or wife who reaches out for their spouse's hand to reconnect, so I reach out to touch God's hand to be reminded that I'm not alone, that someone is experiencing the night with me.

Simplicity, then, is both silence in solitude and detachment in diversion. It ties life together. Simplicity brings eternity into our time and helps us use time for eternity. It gives us strength to do what we must do as citizens of earth but liberates us to live as citizens of heaven.

The Quiet's Reward

The ancients taught that the benefits of simplicity far outweigh the sacrifices it requires. Fénelon wrote that Christians

[24]Ibid., 84–85.

"divest themselves of everything, and in this divesting find a hundredfold return."[25] John of the Cross added, "Oh, if spiritual persons knew how much spiritual good and abundance they lose by not attempting to raise their appetites above childish things, and if they knew to what extent, by not desiring the taste of these trifles, they would discover in this simple spiritual food the savor of all things!"[26]

One of the benefits of simplicity is gaining a new understanding. Thomas à Kempis wrote, "The more a man is united within himself, and becometh inwardly simple, so the more and higher things doth he understand without labor; for that he receiveth intellectual light from above."[27]

The simpler I become, the freer my mind becomes for spiritual understanding and discernment. Clues that flew by me before are now caught and understood. It's as if the "static" is removed so that I can hear the messages more clearly. Perhaps this is what John Climacus referred to when he said "stillness of soul" is "the accurate knowledge of one's thoughts and is an unassailable mind."[28]

Another benefit of simplicity is peace and inner strength. Fénelon said a man with simplicity has a heart with peace that is "deep as the sea in the midst of its troubles."[29]

Today's emphasis on physical prowess betrays our weakness within—we may be spiritual jellyfish but at least we'll have firm abdomens. This focus on bodily fitness is called into question when we remember the ancients' emphasis on inner strength. Teresa of Avila called people who do not know the

[25]Fénelon, *Christian Perfection*, 64.

[26]John of the Cross, "The Ascent of Mount Carmel," in *Selected Writings*, I:5:4.

[27]à Kempis, *The Imitation of Christ*, I:3:3.

[28]Climacus, *The Ladder of Divine Ascent*, 261–62.

[29]Fénelon, *Christian Perfection*, 200.

prayer of quiet "crippled." She wrote, "A very learned man told me that souls who do not practice prayer are like people with paralyzed or crippled bodies; even though they have hands and feet they cannot give orders to these hands and feet. Thus there are souls so ill and so accustomed to being involved in external matters that there is no remedy, nor does it seem they can enter within themselves."[30]

Simplicity, according to Teresa of Avila, is a doorway to prayer, which is also the doorway to inner strength.

Our preoccupation with the momentary and passing things of this world, the goods of the lowest order, keeps us from the better and higher activities we might participate in if we had the time. Financial gurus tell us to spend a month writing down all of our expenses so we can see the waste; a wise spiritual director might have us chart our time and our thoughts for a week so we can see our true priorities.

The point I want to make clear, however, is that simplicity is a freedom, not a burden. If it seems like a burden, we are trying to force our hearts with outward actions and will have only marginal success at best.

Of all the spiritual insights I have gained from reading the classics of the Christian faith, the teaching of simplicity is one of the most precious because of its power to usher us into God's presence.[31] The spiritual life is impossible in a heart full of noise and occupation. God will not fill a heart that has no room.

While simplicity has its own rewards, it still is just a means to an end. It is a filter, not an idol. I seek simplicity only

[30]Teresa of Avila, *The Interior Castle*, I:1:6.

[31]It goes without saying, of course, that this is only possible because of the work Christ has done on our behalf. Simplicity will make any person, even a nonbeliever, stronger, but it cannot save a person's soul.

because God is so great I want to strip away the clutter that keeps me from Him. I am willing to give up all to enter into His precious warmth. Just as we disrobe when the sun casts wide its heat, so we yearn to stand spiritually naked when God's Spirit shines His presence into our souls. We want nothing, absolutely nothing, to stand between us and God because, faced with such beauty, we would be fools to settle for anything less. De Sales exhorted himself, "Since, O my soul! thou art capable of God, woe be to thee if thou content thyself with anything less than God."[32]

Reflections

If simplicity is the true prayer of your heart, copy the following prayer of Thomas à Kempis on a piece of paper:

> O Lord, it is the work of a perfect man, never to relax his mind from attentive thought of heavenly things, and so to pass amid many cares, as it were, without care; not as one destitute of all feeling, but by the prerogative of a free mind, adhering to no creature with inordinate affection. I beseech thee, my most gracious God, preserve me from the cares of this life, lest I should be too much entangled by them; also from the many necessities of the body, lest I should be captivated by pleasure; and from whatever is an obstacle to the soul, lest being broken with troubles, I should be overthrown.[33]

Begin each day with this prayer until it becomes your unconscious yearning. Whenever your heart grows distracted, pull out this prayer and read it again. Just practice turning your heart toward God, using this prayer as a tool, and let God lead you into the joy of simplicity.

[32] de Sales, *Introduction to a Devout Life*, 351.
[33] à Kempis, *The Imitation of Christ*, III:26:1–2.

Chapter Seven

The High and the Low: A Double-Sided Humility

> *Knowing God without knowing our own wretchedness makes for pride. Knowing our own wretchedness without knowing God makes for despair. Knowing Jesus Christ strikes the balance because he shows us both God and our own wretchedness.*   Blaise Pascal
>
> *A proud monk needs no demon. He has turned into one, an enemy to himself.*   John Climacus
>
> *God will give illumination by bestowing on the soul not only knowledge of its own misery and lowliness but also knowledge of His grandeur and majesty.*
> John of the Cross

Augustine, the fourth-century bishop, wore authority like a well-fitting coat. He was a talented and colorful young man, but after his conversion to Christianity and the death of his mother, he was virtually ready to retire. He moved to his birthplace, Tagaste, seeking a life of contemplation and reflection. Such a personality isn't easily missed, however, and Augustine's quiet life was broken shortly thereafter when, during a visit to Hippo, he was ordained a priest. Just five years later he was consecrated bishop of Hippo.

Such a meteoric rise up the ecclesiastical ladder doesn't happen by accident, and Augustine's career verified his calling and the speed of its recognition. His writings and thoughts have left a permanent imprint on the life of the church.

Augustine could have allowed the church to remember him only as the powerful saint, bishop, and church father he became. The details of his early life were quickly forgotten as his career and influence swelled to great heights. If Augustine had just remained silent, he could have been remembered as a figure without spot or blemish, leaving only his influence and theological system to be passed down for future generations.

But Augustine became concerned about the growing gulf between his reputation and the truth of his beginnings. The crowds saw his powerful personality, his expert training in rhetoric and philosophy, and his leadership. But Augustine, himself, remembered a young, willful, and proud man caught in idleness and then immorality, a heretic with an ambitious thirst for fame, and then, finally, a mother's earnest and life-long prayers answered in the conversion of her son.

This human side could have been lost, but Augustine decided to write his confessions and tell the whole story. Ironically, it was this move of humility that helped further launch his fame and establish his place in history as *The Confessions of Saint Augustine* became one of the most widely read Christian books of all time.

Augustine realized what all the saints have realized: Humility and honesty are essential ingredients of the Christian life. Augustine wanted people to see God's greatness, and he realized it is often best revealed through human weakness. Not to tell his whole story would have been to rob God of the glory due Him for the remarkable work of transformation He accomplished in Augustine's life.

The Twin Pillars of Humility: Our Lowliness and God's Greatness

The twin pillars of a truly Christian spirituality are realizing our own lowliness and God's greatness.[1] The spiritual writers speak with virtual unanimity on the need to not just understand, but be shaken in the depths of our being by God's grandeur and our poverty. These twin pillars can be combined into one word: *humility.*

Fénelon wrote, "All the saints are convinced that sincere humility is the foundation of all virtues. This is because humility is the daughter of pure charity, and humility is nothing else but truth. There are only two truths in the world, that God is all, and the creature nothing."[2]

Thomas à Kempis believed humility is the common element of the most mature Christians. "The greatest saints before God are the least in their own judgments; and the more glorious they are, so much the humbler within themselves."[3]

He was joined in this belief by Teresa of Avila, who saw humility as the foundation of our entire spirituality, without which we cannot grow. "And if souls aren't determined about becoming His slaves, let them be convinced that they are not making much progress, for this whole building . . . has humility as its foundation. If humility is not genuinely present, for your own sake the Lord will not construct a high building lest that building fall to the ground. Thus . . . that you might build

[1]John Owen wrote, "Two things are needed to humble us. First, let us consider God in His greatness, glory, holiness, power, majesty, and authority. Then, let us consider ourselves in our mean, abject, and sinful condition" (*Sin and Temptation* [Portland: Multnomah, 1983], 28).

[2]Fénelon, *Christian Perfection*, 205.

[3]à Kempis, *The Imitation of Christ*, II:10:4.

on good foundations, strive to be the least and the slaves of all, looking at how or where you can please and serve them. What you do in this matter you do more for yourself than for them and lay stones so firmly that the castle will not fall."[4]

Early in my Christian life I realized I was trying to use Christianity just as I tried to use tennis or running—to make a name for myself, to have an identity as an extraordinary Christian. I went to great lengths to improve my faith, but it was all for nought. I wish I would have read John Climacus back then, for even though he lived in the monastic world, Climacus still realized that humility, not sacrifice, is at the heart of a true faith: "And there are men who wear out their bodies to no purpose in the pursuit of total dispassion, heavenly treasures, miracle working, and prophetic ability, and the poor fools do not realize that humility, not hard work, is the mother of such things."[5]

Even William Law, who, like Climacus, is known for his strict discipline, writes that humility "is so essential to the right state of our souls that there is no pretending to a reasonable or pious life without it. We may as well think to see without eyes or live without breath as to live in the spirit of religion without the spirit of humility."[6]

There is no truly Christian spirituality without humility. Proud, self-righteous preaching may win crowds and fame, but it has no place in the communion of saints who have been writing about the Christian life for two thousand years. Let's take a closer look at the foundation of Christian humility and its place in the Christian life.

[4]Teresa of Avila, *The Interior Castle*, VII:4:8.
[5]Climacus, *The Ladder of Divine Ascent*, 204.
[6]Law, *A Serious Call*, 228.

It follows that if truth is such an important component of humility, then an accurate self-knowledge is essential.

Christian: Know Thyself!

While some of us hide our true selves behind a glittering image (we'll talk about "spiritual cosmetology" in a moment), others of us simply don't know who we really are. Climacus said, "It happens . . . that most of the proud never really discover their true selves. They think they have conquered their passions and they find out how poor they really are only after they die."[7]

Thomas à Kempis believed that an accurate self-knowledge always leads to humility. "Whoso knoweth himself well, is lowly in his own sight and delighteth not in the praises of men."[8] It follows that if we *aren't* lowly in our own sight and are dependent on the praise of others, then we don't know ourselves very well.

Teresa of Avila drew this out. Like Thomas à Kempis, Teresa equated accurate knowledge with humility. "Knowing ourselves is something so important that I wouldn't want any relaxation ever in this regard. . . . While we are on this earth nothing is more important to us than humility."[9]

This points to a danger hidden in our desire for spiritual growth. We can become so enamored by the person we want to become we lose touch with the person we are. This trap held me back for several years. There was a time in my life when I feared sin so much that I focused almost exclusively on not sinning. Now sin is a very disturbing thing and you

[7]Climacus, *The Ladder of Divine Ascent*, 210.
[8]à Kempis, *The Imitation of Christ*, I:2:1.
[9]Teresa of Avila, *The Interior Castle*, I:2:9.

might well ask what could be wrong with fearing it. The answer is that my fear was so separated from God's grace that I was afraid to take an honest look into my own heart. I thus lost touch with my weaknesses, and the result was pride. I lived in an illusory and self-deceiving "holiness" based on discipline and works while my heart was full of evil attitudes and judgments. God used a period of dryness to reveal the true state of my heart. It was with great interest, then, that I later read these words of John of the Cross:

> In the dryness and emptiness of this night of the appetite, a person also procures spiritual humility, that virtue opposed to the first capital vice, spiritual pride. Through this humility acquired by means of self-knowledge, individuals are purged of all those imperfections of the vice of pride into which they fell in the time of their prosperity. Aware of their own dryness and wretchedness, the thought of their being more advanced than others does not even occur in its first movements, as it did before; on the contrary, they realize that others are better. From this humility stems love of neighbor, for they will esteem them and not judge them as they did before when they were aware that they enjoyed an intense fervor while others did not. These persons will know only their own misery and keep it so much in sight that they will have no opportunity to watch anyone else's conduct.[10]

Notice that John of the Cross said that humility is "acquired by means of self-knowledge." It is for this reason the anonymous author of *The Cloud of Unknowing* urged us to "labor and sweat, therefore, in every way that you can, seeking to obtain for yourself a true knowledge and feeling of yourself

[10]John of the Cross, "The Dark Night," in *John of the Cross: Selected Writings*, ed. and trans. by Kieran Kavanaugh (New York: Paulist Press, 1987), I:12:7–8.

as you are." This is *not* a search for a secular and autonomous self-understanding. It is rather a search based in the awareness that a "lack of knowledge," as the author puts it, "is the cause of a great deal of pride."[11]

Ironically, if our self-understanding is truly born in heaven, it will actually encourage us rather than discourage us. Fénelon wrote: "As the inner light increases, you will see the imperfections which you have heretofore as basically much greater and more harmful than you had seen them up to the present. . . . But this experience, far from discouraging you, will help to uproot all your self-confidence, and to raze to the ground the whole edifice of pride. Nothing marks so much the solid advancement of a soul, as this view of his wretchedness without anxiety and without discouragement."[12]

Once our self-view is no longer tied to our own worth but to the worth ascribed to us in God, we can readily admit our shortcomings and begin working on them while we are encouraged that we are not left alone in our failings.

While some of us may lack an accurate understanding of our true selves, others know their true selves so well that they spend all their energy trying to put up a false front, thinking some people wouldn't accept them if they knew the truth. This false piety is devastating to true spiritual growth.

Spiritual Cosmetology

When we marshal our energy to protect our glittering image and false piety, we rob resources that could be used to address the parts of our lives about which we are ashamed. Pascal wrote, "We are not satisfied with the life we have in

[11]Anonymous, *The Cloud of Unknowing*, XIV:2:5.
[12]Fénelon, *Christian Perfection*, 22–23.

ourselves and our own being. We want to lead an imaginary life in the eyes of others, and so we try to make an impression. We strive constantly to embellish and preserve our imaginary being, and neglect the real one."[13]

When we are ashamed about where we are spiritually, we have two choices: We can create a false front and a glittering image (the spiritual-cosmetology approach), or we can be honest before God, ourselves, and others about our weakness and allow transformation to occur. We will not have the energy or resources to do both; we must choose one or the other.

Galatians 1:10 says that if our motivation is the approval of others, we cannot at the same time be growing in Christ and dedicated to His service. William Law added, "He that acts upon the desire of praise and applause must part with every other principle; he must say black is white, put bitter for sweet, and sweet for bitter, and do the meanest, basest things in order to be applauded."[14]

When we live a lie we eventually lose touch with reality, and our own words condemn us. Our lives become a sideshow and we fail to become whole and integrated people. Spiritual cosmetology is a circus act, an act that has no place in the Christian life.

It is also an act that God will eventually expose if we ever find our way to a healthy community. We conceal, but God wants to heal; and to do that, He must first expose. God, as a God of truth, is also by nature an exposer. Those who walk closely with God often have eyes that can see through pretense. Consider just a few of the exposing gifts of the Spirit mentioned in Scripture, gifts like prophetic utterance,

[13]Pascal, *Pensées*, 270.
[14]Law, *A Serious Call*, 260.

words of knowledge, the discernment of spirits, and interpretation of tongues. God is in the business of making the unknown known.

When Ananias and Sapphira gave a large gift to the Christian community, they were exposed and found guilty of trying to mislead the community regarding the extent of their sacrifice. God found this pretense worthy of death (Acts 5). God hates lies, all lies; His enemy, the devil, is the father of lies (John 8:44). Jesus described Himself as the way, the *truth*, and the life (John 14:6). So it is no surprise that in the model Christian community spoken of by Paul, God's presence will be known by the unbeliever's having "the secrets of his heart . . . revealed" (1 Cor. 14:25 NKJV). God exposes our secrets because concealed sin is a cancer eating away the spiritual life within us. Without humility, we cannot see the face of God.

Spiritual cosmetology is particularly dangerous when humility becomes part of our makeup.

Humility in Ministry

We can pretend we are humble just as we can pretend we are holy, but true humility cannot be manufactured. Humility is rooted in truth, not pretense. Therefore we need an objective standard by which we can judge ourselves, or better, allow God to judge us, and that standard is often how we respond to the accusations and perceptions of others. De Sales wrote, "We often confess ourselves to be nothing, nay, misery itself, and the refuse of the world; but would be very sorry that any one should believe us, or tell others that we are really so miserable wretches."[15]

[15]de Sales, *Introduction to a Devout Life*, 138.

Our protected self-images can be idols, keeping us from effective ministry. We're more concerned about the image than the truth, so we get upset if someone is saying something that causes others to hold a lower view of us—even if that view is true. Does it ever occur to us that people can be healed by stories of our failures as much as they can be healed by stories of our victories?

After I gave a presentation at a church, I noticed a woman who was weeping in one of the front rows as I was answering several questions. After most of the people had left, the woman shared her heart with me. Her Christian son, her pride and joy, had gotten his girlfriend pregnant. Because I still look pretty young, people frequently make a comparison between me and their older children, even though I now have children of my own. I could tell what this woman was thinking, and after we had talked for several minutes she finally put it into words. Through her tears, she said, "As I was listening to your talk and was moved so deeply, I was just thinking how much I wanted my son to be like you—and I thought he could be, until now."

"What makes you think your son can't move on from this?" I asked. "What makes you think he can't learn, even from this, and grow into becoming a strong Christian leader?"

The woman shook her head, but I knew she wasn't convinced. I knew I had a decision to make. I could maintain my glittering image or I could be honest and minister to this woman's needs. "You know, I was in your son's position when I was younger," I told her. The woman's tears became torrents, opening up whole new avenues of conversation and prayer. God used a woman's tears to show me the power of operating in weakness and humility, letting others see me as I am.

We mentioned earlier that Augustine wrote his *Confessions* so people who knew him only as a bishop wouldn't have an overly exalted view of him. When Paul was forced to recite his credentials to the Corinthians, he made sure he ended with a humiliating weakness (2 Cor. 11:22ff.). Throughout history, Christian saints have recognized the need to be transparent. Human weakness points people to the grace and saving power of Christ.

It is one thing to allow people who love us to see our weaknesses, but what about our enemies? When we are attacked, we must avoid what Augustine called the "lust" of vindicating ourselves.[16] According to Augustine, this lust is defeated by a spirit-born humility.

There can be times when we must, however, for holy reasons, speak up in our own defense. Humility allows us to present a defense when doing so is vital to preserving a work that God has called us to do. De Sales wrote, "humility would despise a good name if charity did not need it; but, because it is one of the foundations of human society, and that without it we are not only unprofitable, but prejudicial to the public, by reason of the scandal it would receive, charity requires, and humility consents, that we should desire [a good name], and carefully preserve it." He added, however, that "we must not be over-nice in regard to the preservation of our good name. . . . Persons, by endeavoring to maintain their reputation so delicately, entirely lose it. . . . An excessive fear of losing our good name betrays a great distrust of its foundation, which is the truth of a good life."[17] Humility gives us true freedom.

[16]Augustine, *Confessions*, X:58.
[17]de Sales, *Introduction to a Devout Life*, 148–49.

The Freedom of Humility

Humility is at root a celebration of our freedom in Christ; we are freed from having to make a certain impression or create a false front. Humility places within us a desire for people to know us as we are, not as we hope to be and not as we think they want us to be or even as we think we should be. Real growth cannot begin until we come to this point.

The doorway to humility is acknowledging and then accepting the truth. "Humility does not consist in having a worse opinion of ourselves than we deserve, or in abasing ourselves lower than we really are. But as all virtue is founded in truth, so humility is founded in a true and just sense of our weakness, misery, and sin. He that rightly feels and lives in this sense of his condition lives in humility," says Law.[18]

Humility, then, is simply admitting what is true; it is the dissolution of all pretense, a commitment to honesty and "real reality." Fénelon described it as "a certain honesty, and childlike willingness to acknowledge our faults, to recover from them, and to submit to the advice of experienced people; these will be solid useful virtues, adapted to your sanctification."[19]

This honesty means that we do not try to mislead others as to how holy or advanced we are.[20] Just as we are eager to correct someone's incorrect and negative impression of us, so we should be equally willing to make sure they don't think better of us than is warranted. To try to mislead people re-

[18]Law, *A Serious Call*, 229.

[19]Fénelon, *Christian Perfection*, 90.

[20]"To imagine we know what we do not know is folly; to desire to pass for knowing that of which we are ignorant is an intolerable vanity" (de Sales, *Introduction to a Devout Life*, 141).

garding our true state is to lie to them—a poor basis for a relationship.

Teresa of Avila wrote, "I'm saying that we should walk in truth before God and people in as many ways as possible. Especially, there should be no desire that others consider us better than we are."[21]

Teresa rooted humility in the very nature of God:

> Once I was pondering why our Lord was so fond of this virtue of humility, and this thought came to me—in my opinion not as a result of reflection but suddenly: It is because God is supreme Truth; and to be humble is to walk in truth, for it is a very deep truth that of ourselves we have nothing good but only misery and nothingness. Whoever does not understand this walks in falsehood. The more anyone understands it the more he pleases the supreme Truth because he is walking in truth.[22]

This truth liberates; it is our call to freedom. Christians must know themselves, and they must know their God.

Christian, Know Thy God

Humility contains two truths—the lowness of men and women and the greatness of God. The most proper and healthy way to obtain humility is to view our spark in the perspective of God's great sun.

The author of *The Cloud of Unknowing* wrote that we "should choose rather to be humbled under the wonderful height and worthiness of God who is perfect than under [our] own wretchedness which is imperfect. That is to say, take

[21]Teresa of Avila, *The Interior Castle*, VI:10:6.
[22]Ibid., VI:10:7.

care that your particular attention is directed more to the worthiness of God than to your own sinfulness."[23]

Such an understanding of God's greatness is born in revelation. The gift of truth is God's gift to us. John of the Cross wrote, "God will give illumination by bestowing on the soul not only knowledge of its own misery and lowliness but also knowledge of His grandeur and majesty."[24]

Without a direct experience of God, humility is impossible because our frame of reference is distorted. Fénelon explained, "A peasant shut up in his village only partially knows his wretchedness, but let him see rich palaces, a superb court, and he will realize all the poverty of his village. He cannot endure its hovels after a sight of so much magnificence. It is thus that we see our ugliness and worthlessness in the beauty and infinite grandeur of God."[25]

We've probably all experienced feeling perfectly content with our house and surroundings, and then visited someone who has an extraordinary house or gift at decorating. Then when we return home we find that our furniture suddenly looks like it's lost all its life. Our house didn't change, just our frame of reference. It's easy for a man or woman to be proud until he or she gains a glimpse of the God of the universe. Once we see what could be, humility is as natural a reaction as a child squinting his or her eyes to block out the glare of the sun.

Fénelon said we can use any human measurement we want to reveal our humble state, but such reasoning "only skims the heart. It does not sink in." Only a direct encounter with God

[23]Anonymous, *The Cloud of Unknowing*, XXIII:4.
[24]John of the Cross, "The Dark Night," in *Selected Writings*, I:12:4.
[25]Fénelon, *Christian Perfection*, 145–46.

shakes the depths of our being. "If the ray of the divine light shines within, he sees the abyss of good which is God, the abyss of nothingness and evil which is the corrupted creature."[26]

I have been walking with God now for twenty-five years. It seems I have sung every worship chorus ever written at least a hundred times. I have read the Bible at least a dozen times. I have experienced insights from God that struck me as profound, and the gift of tears as I contemplated the goodness and work of Christ and my own poverty and sin.

But none of that matters for today, and none of that will keep me for tomorrow. This is explained in John Owen's second step in the stages of moral decline and decay: losing reverence for God.[27] I need to be in awe of God *today*. If I ever become too familiar with God, if I ever lose that profound reverence that leaves me standing silent in fascination and wonder, pride and sin will be waiting to claim my soul.

If I want to be humble, I must remain lost in the Great Light. I must be astonished at the depth, breadth, and height of the God I serve. Apart from this understanding, I lose touch with myself and with those around me. I grow too large, and those around me grow too small.

Thus true self-knowledge is found only in relation to God. Teresa of Avila wrote, "We shall never completely know ourselves if we don't strive to know God. By gazing at His grandeur, we get in touch with our own lowliness; by looking at His purity, we shall see our own filth; by pondering His humility, we shall see how far we are from being humble. . . . Something white seems much whiter when next to something black, and vice versa with the black next to the white."[28]

[26]Ibid., 146.
[27]Owen, *Sin and Temptation*, 84–85.
[28]Teresa of Avila, *The Interior Castle*, I:2:9–10.

Consider, please, who is talking. If most people today were to somehow travel back in history and meet Teresa of Avila, their response might be similar to meeting the twentieth century's Mother Teresa of Calcutta. They might think they have found the picture of purity. What need would such a woman have of repentance? Such a woman learns to embrace humility, not by looking left or right, but by looking up. In God's purity, the purest human soul is the meanest, darkest blot.

Keeping sight of God, then, is vital to humility, just as keeping in touch with humility is vital to seeing God. We cannot maintain one without the other. "Christianity is strange," Pascal wrote. "It bids man to recognize that he is vile, and even abominable, and bids him want to be like God. Without such a counterweight his exaltation would make him horribly vain or his abasement horribly abject."[29]

Humility in Community

Christian communities, including Christian families and churches, break down in proportion to the loss of humility of their members. Owen wrote, "The person who understands the evil in his own heart is the only person who is useful, fruitful, and solid in his beliefs and obedience. Others only delude themselves and thus upset families, churches, and all other relationships. In their self-pride and judgment of others, they show great inconsistency."[30]

Accusation is a very dangerous thing—and one of Satan's favorite tools. According to Fénelon, humility is the only anti-

[29]Pascal, *Pensées*, 133.
[30]Owen, *Sin and Temptation*, 29.

dote. "Can we with justice feel contempt for others and dwell on their faults, when we are full of them ourselves?"[31]

Our "strong feelings about the faults of others" is itself a "great fault," Fénelon added later. "It is an arrogance which raises itself above the low estate of mankind. . . . When will you have nothing more to see either in yourself or in others? God, all good. The creature, all evil."[32]

Community is essential for humility because how we treat others is a better test of our humility than how we treat ourselves. Fénelon says:

> If you were in this happy [humbled] state, far from impatiently enduring those who are not, the immense stretch of your heart would make you indulgent and compassionate toward all the weaknesses which shrink selfish hearts. The more perfect we are, the more we get along with imperfection. The Pharisees could not bear the publicans and the women sinners, whom Jesus Christ treated with such gentleness and kindness.[33]

In his blunt style, Thomas à Kempis said, "Do not think that thou hast made any progress, unless thou feel thyself inferior to all."[34] He believed that humility, especially in relation to others, has a very practical and positive effect. "It is not harmful unto thee to debase thyself under all men; but it is very injurious to thee to prefer thyself before any one man."[35]

This is where many of us fail miserably. We are quick to excuse our own sins but vicious in holding other Christians

[31]Fénelon, *Christian Perfection*, 44.
[32]Ibid., 60.
[33]Ibid., 61.
[34]à Kempis, *The Imitation of Christ*, II:2:2.
[35]Ibid., I:7:3.

to the standard of perfection. Francis de Sales said we are "like the partridges in Paphlagonia, which have two hearts; for we have one heart, mild, favorable, and courteous towards ourselves, and another hard, severe, and rigorous towards our neighbor."[36]

When we sin, we explain that we have been under extra stress, that we have been tired, that Satan has been unceasing in his enticements, or that the actions of others were so egregious as to practically force us into a sinful response. But when we see another person sin, these excuses do not come to mind; no, we base our judgment of others on the bottom line—you sinned, therefore you're guilty.

This tendency to excuse ourselves and quickly judge others is proof that pride has gripped our hearts. William Law's words call us to a severe honesty in this regard. "The fuller of pride anyone is himself, the more impatient will he be at the smallest instances of it in other people. And the less humility anyone has in his own mind, the more will he demand and be delighted with it in other people. . . . You must therefore act by a quite contrary measure and reckon yourself only so far humble as you impose every instance of humility upon yourself and never call for it in other people."[37]

When we harshly judge others, we are elevating ourselves to a position that rightfully belongs to God. We do not know a person's full story, and even if we did, we would lack the perfect objectivity and unpolluted sense of justice to render an accurate opinion. Pastors and appointed leaders must make decisions, but it becomes arrogant judgment when we take on the concerns of people who are not accountable to us.

[36]de Sales, *Introduction to a Devout Life*, 254.
[37]Law, *A Serious Call*, 234.

William Law deserves to be quoted at length in this regard. Remember that his book, *A Serious Call to a Devout and Holy Life,* is one of the most demanding spiritual treatises ever written, yet notice the way Law treats sinners:

> No one is of the Spirit of Christ but he that has the utmost compassion for sinners. Nor is there any greater sign of your own perfection than you find yourself all love and compassion toward them that are very weak and defective. And on the other hand, you have never less reason to be pleased with yourself than when you find yourself most angry and offended at the behavior of others. All sin is certainly to be hated and abhorred wherever it is, but then we must set ourselves against sin as we do against sickness and diseases, by showing ourselves tender and compassionate to the sick and diseased.
>
> All other hatred of sin which does not fill the heart with the softest, tenderest affections toward persons miserable in it is the servant of sin at the same time that it seems to be hating it.[38]

When Jesus faced self-righteous hypocrisy He was brutal and unyielding in His confrontation, but when He faced those caught in the misery of sin He often showed a softer face, becoming a Savior who would not break a bruised reed or blow out a smoldering wick (Isa. 42:3). Law says those who are most like Christ will have a ministry like Christ. "This, therefore, we may take for a certain rule, that the more we partake of the divine nature, the more improved we are ourselves, and the higher our sense of virtue is, the more we shall pity and compassionate those that want it. The sight of such people will then, instead of raising in us a haughty contempt or peevish indignation toward them, fill us with such

[38]Ibid., 294.

bowels of compassion as when we see the miseries of a hospital."[39]

Spiritual maturity means we hold ourselves to a high standard while being gracious toward others. When we know we have been forgiven and when we're not cherishing sin in our hearts, it is not difficult to offer a word of healing and grace to others who are struggling. In fact, since we have received healing and grace, it is only natural that we call others out of their sin with the same attitude that Christ used to call us out of our sin.

I remember a conversation many years ago when a fellow believer was railing about the need to loudly confront and proclaim "God's judgment" against various evils in some individuals' lives. I'm all for calling people to holiness, but what bothered me was the manner in which this was being said. "Tell me," I asked her, "when God won you over, was it through judgment or grace?"

"Grace," she replied. "Why do you ask?"

"Just curious," I said. "If it was grace that won you over, why wouldn't you use that to win others?"

Galatians 6:1 exhorts us, "Brethren, if a man is overtaken in any trespass, you who are spiritual restore such a one in a spirit of gentleness" (NKJV).

William Law challenged us to consider where we would be if God treated us like we treat other sinners. "A man naturally fancies that it is his own exceeding love of virtue that makes him not able to bear with those that want it. And when he abhors one man, despises another, and can't bear the name of a third, he supposes it all to be a proof of his own high sense of virtue and just hatred of sin. . . . If this had been

[39]Ibid., 294–95.

the Spirit of the Son of God, if He had hated sin in this manner, there [would have been] no redemption of the world; [if] God had hated sinners in this manner day and night, the world itself [would have] ceased long ago."[40] When we are humble, we may see ourselves as the greatest sinners of all.

The Greatest Sinner

We treat others harshly largely because we don't recognize the depth of our own sin. This is not because of our maturity—after all, the apostle Paul confessed himself to be the chief of sinners. But in an age of widely publicized serial killers, child abusers, drug pushers, and white-collar criminals, many of us might find Paul's sentiments difficult to adopt as our own. We know we have our problems, but Jeffrey Dahmer or Adolf Hitler we're not.

William Law has some helpful words for us in this regard. We may justly condemn ourselves as the greatest sinners we know, he wrote, because we "know more of the folly of [our] own heart than [we] do of other people's," and "the greatness of our guilt arises chiefly from the greatness of God's goodness toward us." Therefore, "every sinner knows more of the aggravations of his own guilt than he does of other people's, and consequently may justly look upon himself to be the greatest sinner that he knows."

Law explained further, "How good God has been to other sinners, what light and instruction he has vouchsafed to them, what blessings and graces they have received from him, how often he has touched their hearts with holy inspirations, you cannot tell. But all this you know of yourself, therefore you know greater aggravations of your own guilt and are able to

[40]Ibid., 294.

charge yourself with greater ingratitude than you can charge upon other people."[41]

Law teaches us that the best way to develop humility is not to compare our life with others', but instead:

> You must consider your own particular circumstances, your health, your sickness, your youth or age, your particular calling, the happiness of your education, the degrees of light and instruction that you have received, the good men that you have conversed with, the admonitions that you have had, the good books that you have read, the numberless multitude of divine blessings, graces, and favors that you have received, the good motions of grace that you have resisted, the resolutions of amendment that you have often broken, and the checks of conscience that you have disregarded.
>
> For it is from these circumstances that everyone is to state the measure and greatness of his own guilt. And as you know only these circumstances of your own sins, so you must necessarily know how to charge yourself with higher degrees of guilt than you can charge upon other people.
>
> God almighty knows greater sinners, it may be, than you are, because he sees and knows the circumstances of all men's sins. But your own heart, if it is faithful to you, can discover no guilt so great as your own, because it can only see in you those circumstances on which great part of the guilt of sin is founded.
>
> You may see sins in other people that you cannot charge upon yourself, but then you know a number of circumstances of your own guilt that you cannot lay to their charge.[42]

If others had had our advantages, they might have been much more faithful than we have been. If we had had their

[41]Ibid., 337.
[42]Ibid., 338.

disadvantages, we might have done much worse. We simply don't know, and therefore we are incapable of accurately judging anyone but ourselves.

The Anchor of Our Calling

The final thing we will say about humility is that it is the anchor of our calling and vocation. Pride can turn us against our own purpose in life by filling us with ambitious yearnings that cause us to neglect our true call for today.

Tomorrow's dreams are a poor substitute for today's obedience. Without humility, however, we can fall prey to deceitful desires that hinder our present effectiveness. Teresa of Avila wrote, "sometimes the devil gives us great desires so that we will avoid setting ourselves to the task at hand, serving our Lord in possible things, and instead be content with having desired the impossible."[43]

Francis de Sales's words are strikingly similar. "The enemy often suggests a great desire of things that are absent, and which shall never occur, so that he may divert our mind from present objects, from which, however trivial they may be, we might obtain considerable profit to ourselves."[44]

It is noble to desire to do great things for God; but when our desire for future ministry blocks us from our present task, we should prayerfully (and with the assistance of spiritual counsel) consider whether the desire is God's inspiration to move or Satan's distraction to keep us from living a fruitful life.

Some Christians who have a true calling to be leaders of

[43]Teresa of Avila, *The Interior Castle*, VII:4:14.
[44]de Sales, *Introduction to a Devout Life*, 257–58.

worship may be neglecting that calling in search of the elusive record contract. Some pastors may be called to minister to waning congregations that, because of geography or demographics, simply aren't going to grow very much, but they neglect their pastoral duties out of their determination to create a megachurch.

Dreams born out of our own ambitions can be demonic messengers disguised as angels of light. Dreams born in the heart of God can be precious motivators. Humility will remind us that our reward before God is not based on what we attempt but on our faithfulness to what we are given. De Sales wrote:

> The King of Glory does not recompense his servants according to the dignity of the offices they hold, but according to the measure of the love and humility with which they exercise them. Saul, seeking the asses of his father, found the kingdom of Israel. Rebecca, watering the camels of Abraham, became the spouse of his son. Ruth, gleaning after the reapers of Boaz, and laying down at his feet, was advanced to his side and made his wife. High and elevated pretensions to extraordinary favors are subject to illusion and deceit; and it sometimes happens that those who imagine themselves angels are not so much as good men. . . .
>
> We must . . . keep ourselves in our lower but safer way, less eminent, but better suited to our insufficiency and littleness; in which, if we conduct ourselves with humility and fidelity, God will infallibly elevate us to a situation that will be truly exalted.[45]

Humility is not only the anchor that keeps us where we should be, however; it is also the wind that takes us where we might otherwise fear to sail. For though some of us use pride to escape the obligations of the present, others use

[45]Ibid., 126–27.

pride to avoid a call to the future. "The proud man, who trusts in himself," de Sales wrote, "has just reason not to attempt anything; but he that is humble is so much the more courageous, by how much the more he acknowledges his own inability; and the more wretched he esteems himself the more confident he becomes; because he places his whole trust in God, who delights to display his omnipotence in our weakness, and to elevate his mercy upon our misery."[46]

When it comes to Christian ministry, we have to avoid the trap of basing our qualification on our person rather than our calling. A person with many gifts is not necessarily qualified because of those gifts; likewise, a person lacking in many gifts is not necessarily disqualified because of that lack. It is pride that moves us to evaluate God's call based on what we possess or what we lack. We forget that both the biggest human contribution and the greatest human weakness are irrelevant in the face of God's infinity. God's unlimited power is neither strengthened by our contribution nor lessened by our weakness.

John the Baptist was the quintessential example of a humble servant of God. He was willing to serve humbly and obscurely in the desert while God readied him for his ministry. He spoke forcefully when God exalted him to become a famous and powerful prophet, but then he willingly handed his ministry over to Christ when the time was right.

May God raise up many more such servants.

Reflections

Read Acts 5:1–11. Is there any area of your life in which you, like Ananias and Sapphira, are pretending to be some-

[46]Ibid., 140–41.

thing you are not? Remember that Ananias and Sapphira gave a great deal—but they pretended to give a greater percentage than they actually did. Do you mislead others into believing you are further along than you really are? Allow God to search your heart.

Read John 8:1–11. When you come face-to-face with someone who has been caught in a sin, do you tend to respond as Christ responded? Or does your response more closely resemble that of the Pharisees? Remember that we are talking about the inner attitude of your heart. Ask God to show you the true state of your attitude toward others, particularly those caught in sin.

Read Luke 14:7–11. Are you faithfully and contentedly serving at the end of the table, or are you presuming on a seat up front? Are you allowing dreams to distract you from today's ministry, or are you exercising your faithfulness in the here and now, content to leave any hope of future advancement in God's hands?

Chapter Eight

Living in a Dying World: The Remembrance of Death

> *We cannot too greatly deplore the blindness of men who do not want to think of death, and who turn away from an inevitable thing which we could be happy to think of often. Death only troubles carnal people.*   Fénelon
>
> *Happy is he that always hath the hour of his death before his eyes, and daily prepareth himself to die.*
>
> Thomas à Kempis
>
> *What message from heaven speak[s] louder to us than the daily dying and departure of our fellow creature does?*
>
> William Law

When a sportscaster died at the age of forty-four in Washington, D.C., the city was in shock for several days; this in a city that has been dubbed the murder capital of the United States, where victims of violent crime die virtually every day, sometimes a half-dozen a night. Radio talk-show hosts devoted entire mornings or afternoons to the sportscaster's death. It was covered every day for a week in the newspaper, through his funeral and beyond. One station even ran a half-hour memorial program in remembrance of the sportscaster.

What affected the city as much as who died was death itself, an unexpected intruder that forced everyone to remember that death doesn't always wait until we're ninety-five. Sometimes it sneaks up on us in our forties.

As people called talk shows to express their shock, one familiar refrain kept repeating itself: "It was so sudden; so unexpected. He was so young, in such good health, and then all of a sudden . . . I just can't believe it."

The sportscaster had recently completed a marathon. He was young, healthy, humorous, and successful, but all of that became irrelevant to the brain tumor. Death didn't take into account his cardiovascular capability. It didn't inquire as to the number of children still depending on him or his vocational success or any number of things that matter to us. Death doesn't ask questions; it doesn't review résumés. It just comes.

What bothered the city was the rudeness of death's intrusion into its life. Denial was no longer possible, and people were forced to consider that maybe, just maybe, there's more to life than we have been told. Maybe we need to make some inquiries and answer a few questions before death comes to knock on *our* door.

Every now and then we sneak a peek at the obituaries and look at the ages of those who have died. When we see somebody our own age or even younger, we involuntarily wince. We grope for the cause of death—please don't be a heart attack, or cancer, we hope. We want to be immune from that, at least for now.

Our denial means nothing to death, since death doesn't have to ask our permission. Death is coming. Every day is somebody's last.

The Denial of Death

In spite of the prevalence of death, we prefer not to talk about it. In this we're not unlike previous generations. Fénelon wrote of this denial centuries ago: "We consider ourselves immortal, or at least as though going to live for centuries. Folly of the human spirit! Every day those who die soon follow those who are already dead. One about to leave on a journey ought not to think himself far from one who went only two days before. Life flows by like a flood."[1]

Most of us recognize that we will eventually die, but this recognition is reserved for a distant event decades from now, not today, not this week, not this month, not this year. Death is a foreigner, not a close neighbor.

We live our lives, clutching fiercely to this illusion. How else can we explain the fact that so many die without a will? We live without making a will, not because we believe we'll never die, but because we don't expect to die this week. Thus we have more important tasks to take care of, meetings to attend, things to buy, decorations to hang.

Why do we deny death? Fénelon believed we avoid the thought of death so we are not saddened by it. But this, he said, is shortsighted. "It will only be sad for those who have not thought about it."[2]

William Law wrote that the living world's brilliance blinds us from eternity and the reality of death. "The health of our bodies, the passions of our minds, the noise and hurry and pleasures and business of the world, lead us on with eyes that see not and ears that hear not."[3]

[1]Fénelon, *Christian Perfection*, 85–86.
[2]Ibid., 104.
[3]Law, *A Serious Call*, 69.

Part of this denial comes from the company we keep. During the seven years I attended college and seminary, I attended a church with a congregation that was predominantly young. During those seven years one person in the congregation died, and it was big news.

My first position after seminary was in a more historic church with a predominantly older congregation. While our other church required two rooms to break up the nursery, this church couldn't have rounded up enough babies to fill more than two or three double strollers. During our first six months there were at least three funerals.

Young people have a distorted view of life. We forget that funerals are waiting on the other end of weddings and baby showers. When we segregate ourselves—when we don't know anyone who is suffering from arthritis—we can be lulled to sleep.

Law insisted that most people will regret delaying the thought of death. When death approaches, it is often too late to make amends, and anything we might have gained from it will be lost. Law demonstrated this by describing a symbolic character who, on his deathbed, bemoans his absentmindedness: "Do you think anything can astonish and confound a dying man like this? What pain do you think a man must feel when his conscience lays all this folly to his charge, when it shall show him how regular, exact, and wise he has been in small matters that are passed away like a dream and how stupid and senseless he has lived, without any reflection, without any rules, in things of such eternal moment as no heart can sufficiently conceive them!"[4]

One writer told the story of a shopper who suffered a

[4]Ibid., 73.

massive heart attack in front of the frozen pizza section of a supermarket. The writer ruminated about the woman's last thoughts. "Should I get pepperoni or vegetarian?" Or maybe, "How about triple cheese?" The shopper was seconds away from eternity, on the threshold of entering a new era, and *she didn't even know it*. Her mind was occupied with the trivial.

It is this unexpectedness of death that should encourage us to take a second look, to reconsider our pleasant denial, to admit that, yes, death might visit us as early as this week.

General William Nelson, a Union general in the Civil War, was consumed with the hostilities in Kentucky when a brawl ended up in his being shot in the chest. He had faced many battles, but the fatal blow came while he was relaxing with his men. As such, he was caught fully unprepared. As men ran up the stairs to help him, the general had just one request: "Send for a clergyman; I wish to be baptized."

He never had had the time as an adolescent or as a young man. He never had found the time as a private or taken the time after he became a general. His wound didn't stop or slow down the war. Everything around him was left virtually unchanged except for the general's priorities. With only minutes left before he died, the one thing he cared about was preparing for eternity. He wanted to be baptized.

Thirty minutes later he was dead.

How was this general served by the remembrance of death? Hardly at all, because he remembered it too late.

To help us avoid such a gross oversight, Thomas à Kempis urged, "Thou oughtest so to order thyself in all thy thoughts and actions, as if today thou wert about to die."[5]

[5]à Kempis, *The Imitation of Christ*, I:23:1.

Law expounded on this: "I can't see why every gentleman, merchant, or soldier should not put these questions seriously to himself: What is the best thing for me to intend and drive at in all my actions? How shall I do to make the most of human life? What ways shall I wish that I had taken when I am leaving the world?"[6]

When we find out we have only thirty minutes left to live, as General Nelson did, we can't do much more than prepare our own souls. Even worse, the moment of death could prove that our whole life has been a lie.

As vice president, George Bush represented the United States at the funeral of former Soviet boss Leonid Brezhnev. Bush was deeply moved by a silent protest carried out by Brezhnev's widow. She stood motionless by the coffin until seconds before it was closed. Then, just as the soldiers touched the lid, Brezhnev's wife performed an act of great courage and hope, a gesture that must surely rank as one of the most profound acts of civil disobedience ever committed.

Brezhnev's widow reached down and made the sign of the cross on her husband's chest.

There, in the citadel of secular, atheistic power, the wife of the man who had run it all hoped that her husband was wrong. She hoped that there was another life and that that life was best represented by Jesus who died on the cross. She hoped that same Jesus might yet have mercy on her husband.

The thought of death came too late for an American Civil War general and a Soviet head of state—will it come too late for us?

[6]Law, *A Serious Call*, 282.

Making Death Our Servant

"Imagine a number of men in chains, all under sentence of death, some of whom are each day butchered in the sight of others; those remaining see their own condition in that of their fellows, and looking at each other with grief and despair await their turn. This is the image of the human condition."[7]

In this quote, Blaise Pascal captured the reality of the human condition, a reality many of us would rather not think about. The ancients found great spiritual benefit in looking death in the face, seizing its reality, and making it their servant. They used death to teach themselves how to live.

Climacus urged Christians to use the reality of death to our benefit. "You cannot pass a day devoutly unless you think of it as your last," he wrote.[8] He called the thought of death the "most essential of all works" and a gift from God.[9] "The man who lives daily with the thought of death is to be admired, and the man who gives himself to it by the hour is surely a saint."[10]

Remembering death acts like a filter, helping us to hold on to the essential and let go of the trivial. Climacus pointed out that a "man who has heard himself sentenced to death will not worry about the way theaters are run."[11] His point, of course, is that all of us have been sentenced to death; it's just a matter of time, so shouldn't we live our lives accord-

[7]Pascal, *Pensées*, 165.
[8]Climacus, *The Ladder of Divine Ascent*, 135.
[9]Ibid., 132.
[10]Ibid., 132–33.
[11]Ibid., 143–44.

ingly? Why let trivia captivate our hearts? Forgetting death tempts us to lose perspective.

Death Focuses Our Perspective

Eternity turns everything around. I'm reminded of this every year when I figure my taxes. During the year, I rejoice at the paychecks and extra income, and sometimes I wince when I write out the tithe and offering. I do my best to be a joyful giver, but I confess it's not always easy, especially when there are other perceived needs and wants.

At the end of the year, however, all of that changes. As I'm figuring my tax liability, I wince at every source of income and rejoice with every tithe and offering check—more income means more taxes, but every offering and tithe means fewer taxes. Everything is turned upside down, or perhaps more appropriately, rightside up.

I suspect Judgment Day will be like that. Those things that bother us now, that force us out of our schedules—taking time out to encourage or help someone, for instance—will be the very things we deem most important. We may not remember the movie we skipped to paint the invalid's house or the meeting we missed to visit that prisoner or sick person, but in eternity we will remember those acts of kindness and love and we'll be glad we took the time to do them.

Death not only filters our priorities, it also filters our passions. Pascal wrote, "To render passion harmless let us behave as though we had only a week to live."[12] Notice the utilitarian element in Pascal's teaching: We remember death "to render passion harmless." All of us are captive to various passions: some good, some bad. Which ones will we follow?

[12]Pascal, *Pensées*, 143.

Law suggested we pick and choose according to how we'll feel upon our death. "The best way for anyone to know how much he ought to aspire after holiness is to consider not how much will make his present life easy, but to ask himself how much he thinks will make him easy at the hour of death."[13]

What man in his right mind would continue contemplating an affair if he really believed he might not wake up in the morning? What person would risk entering eternity in a drunken stupor? What fool would ignore his loved ones and his God for one last night so he could make another quick ten thousand dollars just before he died?[14]

Fénelon called the thought of death "the best rule which we could make for all our actions and undertakings."[15] Thomas à Kempis agreed, arguing that the remembrance of death is a powerful force for spiritual growth:

> Didst thou oftener think of thy death than of thy living long, there is no question but thou wouldst be more zealous to improve. If also thou didst but consider within thyself the infernal pains in the other world, I believe thou wouldst willingly undergo any labor or sorrow in this world, and not be afraid of the greatest austerity. But because these things enter not to the heart, and we still love those things only that delight us, therefore we remain cold and very dull in religion.[16]

When we schedule our priorities and follow our passions without regard to eternity, we are essentially looking into the

[13]Law, *A Serious Call*, 68.

[14]"If a merchant, having forbore from too great business that he might quietly attend on the service of God, should therefore die worth twenty instead of fifty thousand pounds, could anyone say that he had mistaken his calling, or gone a loser out of the world?" (Law, *A Serious Call*, 282).

[15]Fénelon, *Christian Perfection*, 104.

[16]à Kempis, *The Imitation of Christ*, I:21:5.

wrong end of a telescope. Instead of seeing things more clearly, our vision becomes tunneled and distorted. We miss the big picture. Law wrote:

"Feasts and business and pleasures and enjoyments seem great things to us whilst we think of nothing else; but as soon as we add death to them, they all sink into an equal littleness; and the soul that is separated from the body no more laments the loss of business than the losing of a feast."[17]

It is only the denial of death that allows us to continue rebelling against God. It is only because we are presuming on some future time to set things right that we ever even consider letting them go wrong. Some of us will be surprised in our presumption; eventually our spirits will be dulled until we forget we are presuming, and like all the rest, death will catch us by surprise.

That's why Thomas à Kempis urged us, "Labor now to live so, that at the hour of death thou mayest rather rejoice than fear."[18] That hour is coming. If it comes tonight, will you be able to rejoice at your state? Or does the mere thought strike fear into your soul? More is involved than just our eternal destiny. God's mercy may well pass us into His eternal presence, but do we want to enter heaven after faithfully serving God to the best of our ability, or after some desperate, last-minute confession, realizing that we have wasted our lives?

I want to enter death tired. I want to have spent what energy God has apportioned me. The cross-country races that were most satisfying to me were not the ones I won most easily but the ones that took everything I had to win.

[17]Law, *A Serious Call*, 70.
[18]à Kempis, *The Imitation of Christ*, I:23:6.

Weariness produced by hard, diligent labor is a reward, not a curse. An eternal rest awaits all who know Christ, so why are we preoccupied with rest now?

Death becomes our servant, then, when we use it to reorder our priorities and to grow in grace and holiness.

Death Can Be a Comforter

Death can be a consoling thought for those who face particularly difficult losses or trials. Fénelon reminded us, "St. Paul recommends to all Christians that they console themselves together in the thought of death."[19]

Christians, above all people, have reason to be consoled through death. Although we are last on earth, we will be first in heaven. Those who mock our faith and have a sadistic pleasure in polluting our collective soul with their perversion won't have a voice in heaven. The lost loved one we miss so much is waiting for us on the other side of time. Our disabilities or broken-down bodies won't accompany us to heaven. Instead, we'll rejoice as we meet "new and improved" versions of ourselves without the aches and pains and without the propensity to sin.

And even more importantly, death ushers us face-to-face with the cry of our hearts—the one true God—and this is our greatest consolation of all. Any sincere Christian experiences at least a certain degree of loneliness because we long for a more intimate walk with our God—a walk that will be realized beyond our dreams once we pass the threshold of eternity.

It is normal and healthy to experience the pain of death—Jesus, after all, cried at the death of Lazarus—but death can

[19]Fénelon, *Christian Perfection*, 105.

also bring hope, not for what it is, but for what God promises us on the other side. The Christian life doesn't make complete sense without the consoling thought of eternal life. Paul himself said we should be pitied above all if the Christian faith is only for this temporal world (see 1 Cor. 15:19).

Because of Christ, because of the resurrection, because of the goodness and mercy of God, death, our enemy, can be a consoling thought. There will be an end to our struggle for righteousness. A limit has been placed on our pain; our loneliness will not go on forever. Another world is coming, and its glory can lift us up.

Keeping Death Alive

On Wednesdays I occasionally attend a Communion service at an Episcopal church that dates back to the eighteenth century. As is common with many older churches, the building is surrounded by a graveyard. Every Wednesday I must walk through the grave markers on my way in and out.

That short walk does almost as much for me as the service itself. I am reminded as I face the second half of the week that one day, my body, *my* bones, will be lying in the ground. My work on earth will be done. What will matter then? What should matter now in light of that?

I am fond of old graveyards—not in a morbid way, but in a way that inspires me like nothing else. I want to use death the way Thomas à Kempis used it: "Happy is he that always hath the hour of his death before his eyes, and daily prepareth himself to die. . . . When it is morning, think thou mayest die before night; and when evening comes, dare not to promise thyself the next morning. Be thou therefore always in a readiness, and so lead thy life that death may never take thee unprepared."[20]

William Law urged that we make the subject of death the focus of our prayers every evening.

> The subject that is most proper for your prayers [during the evening] is death. Let your prayers therefore then be wholly upon it, reckoning up all the dangers, uncertainties, and terrors of death; let them contain everything that can affect and awaken your mind into just apprehensions of it. Let your petitions be all for right sentiments of the approach and importance of death, and beg of God that your mind may be possessed with such a sense of its nearness that you may have it always in your thoughts, do everything as in sight of it, and make every day a day for preparation for it.
>
> Represent to your imagination that your bed is your grave. . . . Such a solemn resignation of yourself into the hands of God every evening and parting with all the world as if you [were] never to see it anymore, and all this in the silence and darkness of the night, is a practice that will soon have excellent effects upon your spirit.[21]

Another way I keep death alive is by living in the communion of saints. I'll post a picture here or a quote there of someone whose faith and life has encouraged me as a reminder that work has an end. If the world can get by without a Dietrich Bonhoeffer or a Blaise Pascal, it can get by without me—and one day it will. I have a limited time to use, and it may be much shorter than I realize—neither Bonhoeffer nor Pascal made it even into their forties.

When a contemporary saint dies, I live with that person's

[20]à Kempis, *The Imitation of Christ*, I:23:1.
[21]Law, *A Serious Call*, 339–40.

death for weeks. The passing of both Klaus Bockmuehl and F. F. Bruce, just to name two relatively recent examples, gave me great pause and still touch me today. I admire them for what they have done and I thank the God who conquered their rebellion and blessed them with the call to become His sons and servants. Wise shoppers clip coupons. Wise Christians clip obituaries.

But the supreme way for a Christian to keep the thought of death alive is, of course, to remember the crucifixion of our Lord. Every time we take Communion we should do so with the awareness that, just as Christ's work on earth had a beginning and an end (as He ministered in a human body), so the mission He has given us has a beginning and an end. "Death is the destiny of every man; / the living should take this to heart" (Eccles. 7:2b NIV).

Reflections

Have you lived in denial of death? Why? Are you presuming on time in the future to set things right?

Read John 19:30. Do you desire to speak these words upon your death? Are you aware of your calling to a sufficient extent that such a declaration would even be possible?

Read Acts 26:19. What do you have to do to proclaim that you have not been disobedient to God's will for your life?

What can you do to keep the remembrance of death an ongoing reality in your life?

A Difficult I
The Christiaɪ

The more we fear to suffer, the more we need to aɩ
                                                    Fénelon

How many saints has adversity sent to Heaven? And how many poor sinners has prosperity plunged into everlasting misery?   William Law

I would not consider any spirituality worthwhile that wants to walk in sweetness and ease and run from the imitation of Christ.   John Climacus

---

When Mary approached Joseph, she must have been full of wonder as she related what had happened. God had visited her—*her!*—and chosen her and Joseph for an incredible task, raising the Son of God.

How long did it take for Mary's wonder and excitement to slip into confusion and fear when she saw the doubt in Joseph's eyes and heard disbelief from his lips? We're not told about Mary and Joseph's encounter, but it's easy to surmise that Mary knew two things when she left her meeting with Joseph. First, Joseph didn't believe her. He hadn't told her he was planning to break the engagement yet, but she knew that he had serious doubts.

didn't believe her, her life was in dan-
now that the Pharisees weren't slow
ment (death by stoning) for suspected
oseph was a righteous and gentle man,
arisees once Mary's pregnancy began

e questions began? "How can you do
said yes to You, and this is the thanks I
back, only to be called a liar and ridiculed

ave made it so easy on Mary. He could have
rewarded Mary's willingness to bear Jesus by visiting Joseph
before Mary told him about the child. Then Joseph could
have immediately comforted her and said, "It's OK, Mary, I
believe you! God visited me last night and told me all about
it." If Joseph was getting a special visit anyway, why not make
it easy on Mary and visit Joseph a few days earlier?

Maybe God wanted to do a work *in* Mary before He did a
miraculous work *through* Mary. Perhaps. But one thing is
clear. God asked Mary, and He continues to ask His saints,
to travel the difficult road.

The spiritual life has been widely recognized by Christians
as a very difficult life. From Mary to Teresa of Avila (whom
we'll discuss in a moment), obedience always comes with a
price.

The Life of the Cross

Those who have gone before us have left a clear witness:
We may seek God or we may seek ease, but we cannot seek
both. The road we travel is anything but easy. It is true that
God loves us and has a wonderful plan for our lives, but it is

equally true that the plan is often fraught with tension and uncertainty, and with emotional, spiritual, and physical pain.

John Climacus wrote in his book, *The Ladder of Divine Ascent*, "Violence (cf. Matt. 11:12) and unending pain are the lot of those who aim to ascend to heaven with the body, and this especially at the early stages of the enterprise, when our pleasure-loving disposition and our unfeeling hearts must travel through overwhelming grief toward the love of God and holiness. It is hard, truly hard."[1]

Brother Lawrence lived with chronic gout that forced him to walk with a limp. At one point he had to move some barrels, and he did so by rolling them; his physical condition wouldn't allow him to carry them. This was a humbling experience for him. But he didn't spend time writing about his physical condition; to him, the spiritual war was the truly difficult one. "Be not discouraged by the repugnance which you may [feel]. . . . Often, at the outset, one thinks it is lost time, but you must go on, and resolve to persevere in it till death, notwithstanding all the difficulties that may occur."[2]

Brother Lawrence refused to give up. He said in another letter he wrote, "I found no small trouble in this exercise, and yet I continued it, notwithstanding all the difficulties."[3]

The anonymous author of *The Cloud of Unknowing* warned, "A difficult task indeed does he have who commits himself to this work. In fact, it will be exceedingly difficult."[4] He urged his readers to persevere, saying they must "labor

[1]Climacus, *The Ladder of Divine Ascent*, 75.

[2]Brother Lawrence, *The Practice of the Presence of God*, Fourth Letter, 3 November 1685 (Cincinnati: Forward Movement Publications, n.d.).

[3]Brother Lawrence, *The Practice of the Presence of God*, First Letter, undated (Cincinnati: Forward Movement Publications, n.d.).

[4]Anonymous, *The Cloud of Unknowing*, XXVI:1.

in this work with great patience, enduring the pains of it no matter how great they be."[5] If the Christian does not give up, some of this difficulty may ease. "Labor hard for a while, and soon you will find that the difficulty and the pressure of this strenuous work will begin to be eased."[6]

Two Lives, Two Triumphs

Two lives in particular model the place of difficulty in Christian growth. Both Teresa of Avila and John of the Cross faced tremendous adversity but found deep spiritual meaning in their suffering.

Teresa of Avila's classic treatise on prayer, *The Interior Castle*, has inspired millions of Christians to seek a deeper intimacy with God, yet there was a time in Teresa's life when prayer became so painful and difficult that she gave it up altogether.

Teresa entered the Carmelite Monastery of the Incarnation against the wishes of her father. He wanted her to have a good education after her mother died, but he certainly didn't expect her to "throw her life away" by joining a religious order. Teresa had to virtually orphan herself—her mother was dead and she was abandoning her father—to follow God's call on her life. She wrote later that the separation felt like every bone in her body was being sundered.

A few years later, Teresa became very ill and was nearly killed by fantastic methods of treatment. After one "doctor" was finished with her, she slipped into a coma for three days without any signs of life. When she came to, she was partially

[5]Ibid., XXIX:1.
[6]Ibid., XXVI:4.

paralyzed, and three years later, she was still unable to walk.[7]

Her difficulties were more than physical, however. During her thirties, Teresa experienced severe spiritual travail. The woman whose prayer life has inspired so many actually gave up prayer for a short while because her prayer life caused her such pain. She wrote about this period with horror, believing it to be her most serious lapse into sin; but during the time, prayer was so difficult to practice she said she would have preferred heavy penance to prayer. Teresa once wrote to God, "If this is how you treat your friends, it's no wonder you have so many enemies."

Added to the physical and spiritual battles, Teresa soon found herself the cause of an enormous social battle. She wrote *The Interior Castle* while her life's work of founding reformed monasteries was being questioned and threatened by higher authorities. Italian Carmelites feared that Teresa's Spanish reform might spread and compel them to reform themselves. A dear friend of hers, John of the Cross, whom she had put in charge of some of the monasteries she had founded, was viciously treated and thrown into jail for remaining loyal to Teresa's teachings. The social battle may have resurrected Teresa's physical ills, for they once again became intense. Teresa wrote in the prologue of her classic, "I have been experiencing now for three months such great noise and weakness in my head that I've found it a hardship even to write concerning necessary business matters."

Thus, when Teresa of Avila wrote about the difficulties encountered in deepening one's spiritual life, she knew what she was talking about. She said, "What interior and exterior trials the soul suffers before entering the seventh dwelling

---

[7]Biographical information taken from Kieran Kavanaugh's introduction to Teresa of Avila's *The Interior Castle*, 1–5.

place! Indeed, sometimes I reflect and fear that if a soul knew beforehand, its natural weakness would find it most difficult to have the determination to suffer and pass through these trials, no matter what blessings were represented to it."[8]

The "seventh dwelling place" was Teresa's "spiritual marriage" through prayer. When she obtained it, another classic author, John of the Cross, was in the room. What joy these two believers must have felt, for both of them had walked through great difficulty and were now receiving their reward.

John of the Cross, like Teresa, grew up in difficult circumstances. His father died when he was three, and John's family was cast into hunger and poverty. John eventually received a proper education, but still chose to enter a religious order. Because of his connection with Teresa and her teachings, he was arrested, classified as a rebel, and given the usual penalties for such offenses—imprisonment, flogging, and fasting on bread and water. John was kept in a small room, six feet wide by ten feet long, with one tiny, two-inch window for his only source of light. For nine months he lived in darkness with little food and hardly a change of clothing.[9]

Yet a divine light pierced the darkness of that prison cell, and John's teaching on the dark night of the soul has inspired many Christians to persevere through the spiritual desert. Read what John wrote about difficulty: "The darknesses and trials, spiritual and temporal, that fortunate [notice, he says *fortunate*] souls ordinarily undergo on their way to the high

---

[8]Teresa of Avila, *The Interior Castle*, VI:1:1–2. See also John Climacus, *The Ladder of Divine Ascent*, 79: "The Lord has concealed from those in the world the tough, but fine, nature of this struggle. Indeed, if people really understood it, no one would renounce the world."

[9]Biographical details about John of the Cross are taken from Kieran Kavanaugh's introduction to *John of the Cross: Selected Writings*, II:7:8.

state of perfection are so numerous and profound that human science cannot understand them adequately."[10] He added later, "Both the sense and the spirit, as though under an immense and dark load, undergo such agony and pain that the soul would consider death a relief."[11]

Remember, John's life was not easy, but he didn't mention the physical pain, the cold, the hunger, or the loneliness. Instead, he was concerned about the difficult war within, the battle for his soul. This was the struggle he focused on.

In John's mind, internal pain became the "doorkeeper" to further growth. He wrote that often souls do not advance because they are unwilling to face the "dark night" that would lead to a closer walk with God.[12]

John warned of unwise counselors who do not understand the necessity of difficulty. He predicted that those who suffer "will meet someone in the midst of the fullness of their darknesses, trials, conflicts, and temptations who, in the style of Job's comforters, will proclaim that all of this is due to melancholia, depression, or temperament, or to some hidden wickedness, and that as a result God has forsaken them. Therefore the usual verdict is that these individuals must have lived an evil life since such trials affect them."[13]

The counselor may then urge a general confession of sin, which John called, "another crucifixion." He said, "The director does not understand that now perhaps is not the time for such

[10]John of the Cross, "The Ascent of Mount Carmel," in *Selected Writings*, prologue, 1.

[11]John of the Cross, "The Dark Night," in *Selected Writings*, II:5:6.

[12]For a similar opinion, see *The Cloud of Unknowing*, LVI:2: "I maintain that whoever will not go the hard way to heaven will go the easy way to hell."

[13]John of the Cross, "The Ascent of Mount Carmel," in *Selected Writings*, prologue, 4.

activity. Indeed, it is a period for leaving these persons alone in the purgation God is working in them, a time to give comfort and encouragement that they may desire to endure this suffering as long as God wills, for until then, no remedy—whatever the soul does, or the confessor says—is adequate."[14]

When we find ourselves rejecting difficulty, we may find that we are really rejecting the cross—and therefore Christ Himself. It was not just John of the Cross who wrote about this. Consider Thomas à Kempis's words: "Christ's whole life was a cross and martyrdom; and dost thou seek rest and joy for thyself? Thou art deceived, thou art deceived, if thou seek any other thing than to suffer tribulations; for this whole mortal life is full of miseries, and signed on every side with crosses. And the higher a person hath advanced in spirit, so much the heavier crosses he oftentimes findeth."[15]

Willingness to bear the cross results in our spiritual growth, just as surely as a refusal to bear the cross keeps us from growing. Both Teresa and John must have been tempted to turn back many times. They were comforted, however, with the knowledge that throughout Scripture, those who followed God most closely, Christ being the supreme example, suffered most severely. Teresa writes, "We have always seen that those who were closest to Christ our Lord were those with the greatest trials."[16]

Still a Difficult Road

When you travel a lot, everything starts to look the same, so you notice when something out of the ordinary appears—

[14]Ibid., prologue, 5.
[15]à Kempis, *The Imitation of Christ,* II:12:7.
[16]Teresa of Avila, *The Interior Castle,* VII:4:5.

something like a professional-looking man walking with a brief-case in one hand and a colorful pillow in the other hand. When I saw this man on an airplane I decided one half of him looked like he was headed for IBM while the other half looked like he was visiting Camp Chickamauga.

The man explained to the person next to him as we were getting off the plane, "Hotel pillows are always too hard, so I can never get any sleep."

When I think of the cells the ancients lived and slept in, and the innerspring mattress supporting me at night, I wonder if I can ever truly appreciate the ancients' teaching on diffi-culty. The man on the plane couldn't bear a pillow that wasn't fluffed just right. How middle-class American life has softened us!

This morning, I traveled to work from a climate-controlled house in a climate-controlled car to a climate-controlled office. I have virtually no physical pain at this point in my life, and I've never experienced true hunger.

Though Christ says I must be willing to do so, I've never been forced to choose between my family or my vocation and my faith. In fact, my vocation is directly tied to my faith. Growing up, I was occasionally ridiculed for my beliefs, but in my world today, heavily populated by Christian coworkers and Christian conferences, I am usually inspired rather than discouraged whenever I venture outside my office.

Thus, when Scripture and the ancients talk about the diffi-culty of the Christian life, it almost seems melodramatic. Sure, it was difficult for Richard Baxter, who wrote *The Saints' Everlasting Rest* with a grotesque-sized tumor hanging on his body; of course it was difficult for Brother Lawrence, whose painful, chronic gout eventually developed into an ul-cerated leg, leaving him to walk for the rest of his life with a pronounced limp (in a world without cars, wheelchairs, or bikes). Obviously it was difficult for someone like John Climacus, who lived in a monastic world that glorified such practices as perching for decades on sunbaked pillars, constructing living cells that were too small for the monk to ever stand up or lie down, or cultivating leeches on their bodies—after all, they intentionally made it difficult. But is it that difficult for you and me?

If these saints came into a church today, with our padded pews and climate-controlled classrooms, our acoustically perfect sanctuaries, our luxury cars parked in the parking lot—would they still teach that the Christian life is difficult? Would they still say it is "hard, very hard" to follow Christ?

In some ways, they might say it is even harder. When Baxter wrote his famous treatise on heaven, every time he looked down and saw his tumor he was reminded that heaven was drawing near. It was easy for him to be enamored with heaven—his body wouldn't let him forget it. Our surgical and medical advancements lull us into a false security, causing us to forget that we are one missed heartbeat away from heaven. When life becomes easier, faith, to the secular mind, becomes less important.

The physical and social luxuries of our world also make it more difficult for us to face the hard internal issues because we don't have to—there are plenty of escapes. Radios, newspapers, televisions, and videos keep our minds occupied from 6 A.M. to midnight; the weightier thoughts of Christian commitment and sacrifice never need to bother us. We can literally hide from the truth of the Gospel and our responsibility to serve God by filling our lives with noise.

Maybe the luxurious world in which middle-class Christians live assaults our faith every bit as much as the deprivation of the Middle Ages. Former saints had nowhere to turn but to God; we can take our pick.

And while our external world is miles apart from the ancients', the internal world remains the same. Unbelief, sin, and temptation are no less numerous for us, and perhaps even more numerous than they were for our spiritual ancestors. The ancients' message that the Christian life is difficult is every bit as relevant today as when it was first spoken by Christ. We're just a little less willing to embrace it. How do we talk about the cross to a generation that finds unfluffed pillows intolerable?

Converts or Disciples?

The Christian faith contains two elements—good (joy and peace) and bad (pain and suffering)—that our society sees as inherently contradictory. Herein lies the temptation to transform the faith in order to make it more palatable.

When the goal is to make converts rather than disciples, we are tempted to restate the Christian life according to felt needs—the peace, fulfillment, and purpose that life in Christ brings. But speaking of these things exclusively is similar to telling somebody what it feels like to win a gold medal at the Olympics—the accomplishment, joy, and elation—without mentioning the grueling training that must take place to get there.

Scripture says the disciples "strengthened" or "encouraged" each other with the words, "we must through many tribulations enter the kingdom of God."[17] Notice Scripture doesn't say they "threatened" each other with the possibility of suffering. No, they encouraged and strengthened each other.

[17]Acts 14:22 (NKJV).

Jesus chose to compare the way of Christianity with the cross, a brutal executioner's tool leading to the darkness of the tomb, not a gentle instrument leading to hours of ease. (Have you ever heard of a padded, air-conditioned cross?) Such was Christ's introduction to the Christian life when He said, "If anyone desires to come after Me, let him deny himself, and take up his cross daily, and follow Me."[18]

There are at least three reasons why we shouldn't avoid the existence of difficulty in our teaching. The first reason is the most compelling one: We have an obligation to mention the difficulty of the Christian life because Jesus, the Author of our message, mentioned it. We have no right to bear any other message because the Christian faith, for all who follow after Christ, is meant to be unoriginal. It has been given to us. We didn't create it, nor were we given permission to edit it. To transform it in any way is arrogant presumption at best and prideful blasphemy at worst.

Second, when we ignore difficulty we threaten to create disillusioned Christians who jump in the faith with enthusiastic joy but take the next religion out as soon as the joy transforms itself into frustration and struggle. They may eventually abandon the faith altogether and thereby be "inoculated" against real Christianity, mistakenly believing they have "already tried it," when, in fact, they experienced nothing more than a caricature.

Third, we need to remember the difficulty so we can keep going. When we struggle, we need to know others struggle too. Thomas à Kempis wrote, "It is but little which thou sufferest, in comparison with those who suffered so much, who were so strongly tempted, so grievously afflicted, so

18Luke 9:23 (NKJV).

many ways tried and exercised. Thou oughtest therefore to call to mind the heavier sufferings of others, that so thou mayest the easier bear thy own very small troubles."[19]

When we fall, we need to know we are not the first, nor will we be the last. This does not cause us to give any less effort. On the contrary, since we know the Christian life is difficult, whenever difficulty arises we know we are on the right path and we use the difficulty as an encouragement to press on.

God's wonderful plan has a painful beginning and many difficult hills to climb before we reach the final resting ground. We are less than honest when we fail to mention this. Ignatius stated it this way (imagining Christ speaking), "Whoever, therefore, desires to come with Me must labor with Me, in order that following Me in pain, he may likewise follow Me in glory."[20]

The Reality of Human Existence

Why is the Christian life so difficult? Five very difficult and ongoing obstacles plague us. No matter how mature we become, these obstacles unceasingly pursue us whether we are ordained ministers or recent converts. They are part of the natural human condition and we will bear them, to a greater or lesser degree, until we are ushered into eternity.

1. Physical Disabilities and Limitations
(Rom. 8:18–25)

These physical bodies we live in, so necessary and yet so burdensome, are the very first obstacles that slam into our

[19]à Kempis, *The Imitation of Christ,* III:19:1.
[20]Ignatius Loyola, *Spiritual Exercises,* 34.

spiritual idealism. We want to pray but we fall asleep. We desire to fast but our stomachs rage and urge us to break down before the hunger. We want to be patient but the stress we are under leads us to lose our temper.

We are physical beings, subject to all the limitations that such an existence represents. We have to earn a living. We have to face pain, from arthritis to cancer. We grow tired. We get hungry. We fight physical compulsions and fears. These all proceed from the fall of man; until Christ's return, we will live in a broken world.

Our bodies are part of us. Even in our glorified state we will not be bodiless. We will have glorified bodies, yes, but bodies nonetheless. In the meantime, we have to make do with less than perfect instruments through which to live out our faith.

Physical difficulties include financial difficulties. Taxation has increased to such an extent that a Christian who is committed to tithing is virtually committed to living on less than half of his or her income (40 to 50 percent total taxation results if you combine federal, state, and local taxes—plus a 10 percent tithe).

Add this stress to the sinus problems, allergies, headaches, arthritis, and any other ailments we may have, and some days can feel pretty long.

When we sense a spiritual breaking point in our own lives, we need to look at our physical condition. Have we pushed it too far? We shouldn't allow our bodies to master us, but neither should we try to live as if our bodies don't need care. "The soul has no thought or passion but the body is concerned in it; the body has no action or motion but what in some degree affects the soul."[21]

[21]Law, *A Serious Call*, 215.

While physical pain may be a part of the fall, God can and does use it for our spiritual advancement. Brother Lawrence said God "sometimes permits the body to suffer to cure the sickness of the soul."[22]

2. Social Pain (1 Thess. 2:2)

In addition to pain arising from our fallen physical condition, pain is also generated from living in a fallen social environment. We live as sinners surrounded by sinners. People hurt us; our parents, our friends, and our fellow believers all contribute to our pain.

Some of this pain may be deserved; much of it may not be. But the fact is, people are all around us with various neuroses, obsessions, and unhealthy attachments and needs. This social pain often sends us reeling and begging for deliverance, but often we just have to go through it.

My children have a favorite book about going on a bear hunt. A father and his children face all kinds of obstacles—a deep, dark forest; oozing mud; a swirling, whirling snowstorm. At each dilemma they always conclude, "We can't go over it, can't go around it. Oh, no! We have to go through it!"

This book holds a lesson for adults as well as children; we can't always run from social pain, sometimes we just have to go through it. We may be forced to work with unhealthy people. Some might even be married to a cruel spouse or be the child of a cruel parent or the parent of a cruel child. If we run, we'll often end up with the same pain in a different situation. A friend of mine was locked into a difficult relationship with her boss but refused to leave because, she said,

[22]Brother Lawrence, *The Practice of the Presence of God*, Fourteenth Letter (Cincinnati: Forward Movement Publications, n.d.).

"I've had four bosses and they've all been like my current boss. There's no use running. I just have to learn whatever it is God wants to teach me."

When social pain becomes intense we will be tempted to dull the pain with unholy methods—the spiritual quicksand of addictions, food, gambling, television or any of the hundred diversions we use to escape from the pain rather than learn from it—or become bitter and angry at God, insisting that He's not being fair. Our anger may be deeply buried, but healing will begin only when we're willing to accept that life is difficult.

Looked at in this way, divorce becomes spiritually suicidal. Many of the marital situations described as doomed because of "irreconcilable differences" could be the seedbed of growth if we would stay in them and not give up.

It is not a coincidence that Jesus chose twelve disciples who would naturally have problems with the beliefs, attitudes, or dispositions of the others. If I were seeking peace and harmony, I certainly wouldn't put a tax collector with a zealot—two natural enemies. But Jesus knew that real spirituality is proven in our relationships with others and He was willing to call people into relationships that would put them beyond their comfort level.

3. The Tendency to Sin (Rom. 7:14–20)

We are born in sin, and every inclination of our hearts is to do evil. According to John Owen, the rule of sin is broken in believers, and its strength is weakened and impaired, but the law of sin is still "of great force and efficacy." He wrote, "indwelling sin is an exceedingly effective power in believers, working constantly toward evil."[23]

[23]Owen, *Sin and Temptation*, 5.

Thus, Owen wrote, our enemy is not only upon us, but it is also *in us*.[24] We can pretend we are above sin, but such pretending serves Satan, not God. Ignorance of the law of sin, wrote Owen, "breeds senselessness, carelessness, sloth, self-sufficiency, and pride—all of which the Lord's soul abhors."[25]

Paul felt his tendency toward sin keenly when he cried out, "O wretched man that I am!" Notice Paul said, *"I am."* He did not say, "I was," signifying his pre-conversion days. Paul testified he served the law of God with his mind, but his flesh served the law of sin (Rom. 7:24–25 NKJV).

Not that long ago, I was concerned about a local political race. As I read a news story about the other side's candidate, a very funny, sarcastic, and cutting letter to the editor came to my mind. I realized I could embarrass and humiliate the candidate and have a lot of fun doing it.

God has given me a gift of communication, but He lent that gift to bring healing, not to tear others down. I laughed the entire hour it took me to write the letter and get the punch lines just right, then almost cried afterward when God made it very clear to me that I simply could not send it.

How many of us have used a gift God has given us to serve Satan's ends rather than build God's kingdom? How many of us have been given the gift of making money and then let that money waste away on selfish pursuits? How many of us have been gifted with serving, but perverted that gift of service by trying to make others feel indebted to us? How many of us have been given the gift of leadership and then turned that gift into a tool of manipulation and control? If we forget the

[24]Ibid., 7.
[25]Ibid., 9.

law of sin in our lives, if we forget how very difficult it is to obtain mastery over it, Satan will have a field day with our self-righteous carelessness. Even our strengths can become weaknesses if we're not careful.

I know I am called to be perfect and holy, but my inclination is to do evil and be selfish. This creates more than mere difficulty in my life; it can result in a virtual internal war. It's healthy for Christians to be somewhat suspicious of themselves; we have reason to be!

4. Tempted to Sin (1 Pet. 5:8)

The fourth difficulty builds on and exacerbates the third. It is difficult enough having a natural tendency toward sin, but our situation is even worse. We also have a real, living being tempting us to sin, the evil one called Satan. Peter warns us that our "adversary the devil walks about like a roaring lion, seeking whom he may devour" (1 Pet. 5:8 NKJV).

Climacus reiterated that fact. "There are demons to assail us after our renunciation of the world."[26] Satan doesn't watch us give our lives to Christ and then retire in frustration. He continues to try and trip us up. When we pray, he seeks to distract us. When we should be serving, he tempts us to think only of ourselves. He and his minions will do whatever it takes to slow us down or take us off the path entirely.

Since I'm involved in a national ministry, I regularly talk and visit with Christians all over the nation in various situations. The most dangerous Christians are those who have forgotten their tendency to sin—and Satan's agenda to capitalize on that tendency. When Satan is allowed to move in the shadows, forgotten and without restraint, his power can be

[26]Climacus, *The Ladder of Divine Ascent*, 81–82.

tremendous. Thoughtful Christians have never forgotten that we have an enemy as well as a Savior.

It is difficult to gain mastery over the law of sin, and it is difficult to be ever vigilant against the devil's schemes. As Christians, we're going to fail. Our spouses and children are going to fail. Our pastors and fellow church members are going to fail. Someone, right now, is tempting them to fail. We can either admit the difficulty, become a people of grace, and support each other, or we can tear each other apart for the slightest infraction.

I'm not suggesting we downplay the seriousness of sin. I am suggesting, however, that we drop the accusing voice, stop pretending we're above temptation, and learn the biblical admonition to restore people gently (see Gal. 6:1).

Surprisingly enough, the ancients found some measure of comfort in the difficulty of satanic opposition. Climacus, who warned of the reality of demonic opposition, also reminded us that being shot at is evidence that we are fighting. The Christian should not fear this difficulty—it is a sign of progress. Instead we should fear the lack of opposition, for its absence means the enemy has found us unworthy of opposition.

5. A Deceitful Heart (Jer. 17:9)

The heart is deceitful above all things. "There is a way that seems right to a man, / But its end is the way of death" (Prov. 14:12 NKJV). Consider this: Not only do we face the difficulty of physical pain and limitations, not only must we persevere in spite of social pain, not only must we struggle with a tendency to sin, and not only do we face a fierce enemy who tempts us to sin, but all these struggles are played out in an arena in which we walk naturally blind. We deceive ourselves. Sometimes, we become our own enemy.

John Owen wrote that "we do not . . . know the secret intrigues and schemes, twists and turns, actions and tendencies of our own hearts."[27] We are easily led astray, often because we want to be led astray. We confuse our emotions or our fears as the voice of God. We rationalize that God will understand. We pretend the situation we face is ambiguous. We lie to ourselves and others and take the easy road. We run a hundred red lights and then wake up surprised that we have crashed.

We cannot trust ourselves to live the Christian life. The smug, self-confident, and solitary Christian is the deceived Christian who is waiting to fall or who is in the midst of a fall and doesn't know it.

This is why I am so pleased to have mature Christians with whom I pray regularly and who can speak God's truth into my life. They know me well enough to detect even a hint of insincerity in my prayers, and they love me enough to mention it.

Even Paul recognized that he wasn't up to judging himself. "My conscience is clear, but that does not make me innocent" (1 Cor. 4:4 NIV). We have been placed in the toughest battle of our lives only to find that we are to be feared as much as the enemy. Even our own minds, hearts, and spiritual understanding cannot be trusted.

Through the ages, the difficulty of the Christian life has led believers to try many different living arrangements, but three gained the most prominence: solitary living (hermits), a large community of monks living under an abbot (cenobim),

[27]Owen, *Sin and Temptation*, 11.

and small groups in close-knit families living under the guidance of a spiritual father or mother (often called the "middle way"). At various points in his life, John Climacus lived in all three, but eventually settled on the middle way. He found that in solitude he could easily be deceived, as we've discussed here. In a large community he could easily be led astray or pretense could reign (people can pretend in a large group). For him, a small community provided the best mix of accountability and authenticity.

Too many Christians forget this fifth difficulty—the difficulty of self-deception—and take no steps toward protecting themselves against it. Just remember that a solitary Christian is Satan's favorite toy. When we're alone, he'll have the time of his miserable life leading us forward into destruction.

We're Not Done Yet

All right, you might be thinking, the Christian life is difficult, but let's get on with it; this is getting a little uncomfortable.

But wait. We're not done yet. It gets even more difficult. What usually happens when we Christians reach our twenties or thirties? We get married. Now these five realities are doubled. Not only must we deal with difficulty in our own lives, but we must also face our spouses' physical pain, which we must sometimes bear; our spouses' social pain, which we will sometimes pay for; our spouses' tendency to sin, which we will bear the brunt of; and our spouses' assaults from the devil. And our spouses, like us, may not even realize what is going on.

Hold on. That does sound difficult, but I'm still not done. When people get married, they have a tendency to bear children. Pretty soon there are four or five people who face a difficult life, who must endure physical pain and spiritual temptation, and who can bring out the best or worst in each other.

Is it any wonder that some Christians feel beaten up? Is it a surprise that some families simply give up?

The answer is not to give up, of course, but when we don't teach the reality of difficulty, who can blame them for thinking maybe they ought to trade in their family for a new one? They don't realize that they can't run from the human condition, because all they see on Sunday morning are smiling faces that seem impervious to the human condition.

Life is difficult, and the Christian life is even more difficult. Some creative theology has arisen to explain the difficulty away, but a new coat of paint will only hide the pain for a short time. Sooner or later we'll have to face the truth, as à Kempis noted: "If thou bear the cross cheerfully, it will bear thee, and lead thee to the desired end, namely, where there shall be an end of suffering, though here there shall not be. If thou bear it unwillingly, thou makest for thyself a new burden, and increasest thy load, and yet notwithstanding thou must bear it. If thou cast away one cross, without doubt thou shalt find another, and that perhaps a heavier one. Thinkest thou to escape that which no mortal man could ever avoid? Which of the saints in the world was without crosses and tribulation?"[28]

Difficulty as Our Teacher

Difficulty teaches us to be pastoral people, something that does not come naturally to us. If we deny our own pain, we

[28]à Kempis, *The Imitation of Christ*, II:12:5–6.

must also blind ourselves to the pain of others. We also need difficulty because without it we become proud, self-centered, and uncaring monsters who are full of ourselves. I used to be a vicious discipler. I never missed a quiet time, and if someone I was working with did, I questioned the sincerity of his or her faith. Then God in His mercy crushed me for eight long years. Sins I had never faced before came roaring to life. Prayer became difficult. Ministry felt strained and awkward; there was no sense of God's power coursing through me.

At the end of this period a door flew open, the darkness was lifted, and I was changed. I realized God didn't need someone who could preach better than anyone else or who could fast longer, pray more, or evangelize more. He wanted somebody who would love His people. I knew a lot about discipline and commitment, but I knew nothing about love.

Difficulty is not to be feared or denied; it is to be used. I've never heard someone say, "It was only after I made my first million that I finally understood the meaning of life, that my priorities were put in order, and my relationship with God was deepened." But how many of us have heard someone say, "As much as I dislike the disease and the treatment, this cancer (or this unemployment or this betrayal) has taught me a lot about life?"

The absolute demand for ease and comfort is unrealistic; it is Satan's lie and temptation to make us bitter toward God. It is also a request for God to allow us to remain shallow and unrooted in our personalities and our faith. When we learn to see difficulty as the path of growth, our relationships will change. When difficulty is seen as something that can be positive, "hard" relationships become a vital part of Christian spirituality. Difficult work, church, and family relationships—

all can be treasures if we place them in God's hands. Don't run from a relationship simply because it is hard; there are many reasons relationships should end, but mere difficulty is not one of them.

The Sweet Side of Suffering

Sometimes our difficulty is such a heavy burden that we need to be "diligently prepared," as Thomas à Kempis said, "both in mind and by habit."[29] But often, as Teresa of Avila pointed out, the benefits of difficulty soon become so obvious that the pain becomes precious.

"Lord, how you afflict your lovers! But everything is small in comparison to what you give them afterward. It's natural that what is worth much costs much. Moreover, if the suffering is to purify this soul . . . it is as small as a drop of water in the sea. . . . The soul feels that the pain is precious; so precious—it understands it very well—that one could not deserve it. . . . With this knowledge, the soul suffers the pain very willingly and would suffer it all in life, if God were to be thereby served."[30]

This apparent irony, the sweetness of suffering, is widespread in Christian spirituality. Climacus wrote, "If individuals resolutely submit to the carrying of the cross, if they decidedly want to find and endure trial in all things for God, they will discover in all of them great relief and sweetness."[31]

The key to understanding the sweetness of suffering is a will fully submitted to the sovereignty of God, and a clear understanding that, as Paul wrote, "our light affliction, which

[29]Ibid., III:19:2.
[30]Teresa of Avila, *The Interior Castle*, VI:11:6.
[31]Climacus, *The Ladder of Divine Ascent*, 96.

is but for a moment, is working for us a far more exceeding and eternal weight of glory" (2 Cor. 4:17 NKJV). The difficulty is temporary; the benefit is eternal.

"The more the flesh is wasted by affliction, so much the more is the spirit strengthened by inward grace," wrote Thomas à Kempis. "And sometimes he is so comforted with desire of tribulation and adversity, for the love of conformity to the cross of Christ, that he would not wish to be without grief and tribulation; because he believes that he shall be unto God so much the more acceptable, the more and heavier things he can suffer for him."[32]

There is something about an absolute demand for comfort, even in the littlest things, that wrecks our communion with God. My natural man tells me I have a right to live in total comfort, so whenever this comfort is threatened because the climate control malfunctions or life circumstances push back a meal for an hour or two, I get a true picture of the demandingness of my heart and the bitterness and anger that cause my spirit to growl, like an untamed beast, at the slightest discomfort or inconvenience.

I am learning the need to benefit from discomfort, to allow myself at times to go hungry or be cold and learn from the experience, rather than crying for deliverance. Dietrich Bonhoeffer wrote that if we do not have some of the ascetic in us we will find it hard to follow Christ. Difficulty—or to use spiritual language, the cross—has always been a part of Christian spirituality and always will be. Being full and comfortable rarely leads me to remember God, but it is amazing how hard it is to forget Him when I am fasting.

In the history of the church the desire for suffering at times

[32] à Kempis, *The Imitation of Christ*, II:12:8.

became unbalanced, but today we may have gone too far the other way. Fénelon provides a healthy balance: by reminding us that we are not to seek difficulties, but when they come, we should "never let them go by without result."[33]

The sweetness of pain can woo us from the world if we are determined to learn from it rather than complain about it. Teresa of Avila wrote, "The soul is left with greater contempt for the world than before because it sees that nothing in the world was any help to it in that torment, and it is much more detached from creatures because it now sees that only the Creator can console and satisfy it."[34]

The Christian life will not be easy, but there is glory up ahead. The Christian life is not simple, but it is profound. It is not full of ease, but it is more than worth the effort. For when the love of Christ grips our hearts, there is nothing we will not suffer for His sake, no difficulty we will not endure, no trial so long that we refuse to persevere.

Reflections

Consider one of the most difficult challenges of your life. Was God able to use that time for your benefit? If you are in the midst of a particularly difficult time, console yourself by remembering how God has used difficulty for good in the past.

Which of the five elements of difficulty are most troublesome for you? How has the teaching of the spiritual classics helped you to face this difficulty?

Are you in a difficult relationship? What can you learn about yourself and the other person by persevering rather than running? Is there a relationship you need to renew?

[33]Fénelon, *Christian Perfection*, 93.
[34]Teresa of Avila, *The Interior Castle*, VI:11:10.

Chapter Ten

Spiritual Gluttony:
Spiritual Feelings

It is very expedient for thy welfare, that thou be left sometimes without taste of spiritual sweetness, and in a dry condition, lest perhaps thou shouldest be vain about thy prosperous estate, and shouldest be willing to please thyself in that which thou art not.   Thomas à Kempis

There [is] need of fidelity in those times of dryness . . . by which God tries our love for Him.   Brother Lawrence

Sometimes you shall find yourself so absolutely destitute of all feeling of devotion that your soul shall seem to be a wild, fruitless, barren desert, in which there is no trace of a pathway to find her God, nor any water of grace to refresh her, on account of the dryness which seems to threaten her with a total and absolute desolation.   Francis de Sales

From his earliest youth, Francis de Sales appeared destined to become a great saint. He was involved in the occasional boyish prank, but he never approached the worldliness of, say, a young Ignatius or Augustine.

What particularly set Francis off from his contemporaries was his unusual spiritual sensitivity. Between his eighteenth and nineteenth year, Francis's sensitive soul became tormented by a vicious temptation toward despair. "A morbid conviction grew upon him that he was destined by God for damnation—and naturally enough, this neurotic nightmare quickly induced an invalidism of body and soul."[1] No one seemed to be a more unlikely candidate for eternal damnation, but you couldn't convince Francis of that.

Francis lived with this torment for several weeks until he was able to pray, "If I may not love Thee in the other world—for in hell none praise Thee—let me at least spend every moment of my brief life here in loving Thee as much as I can." After this prayer left his lips, every trace of Francis's spiritual disease "fell at his feet like the scales of a leper." According to biographer Katherine Bregy, "the only legacy of his anguished temptation was to be in ever patient sympathy with other tortured souls."

In my reading of spiritual biographies and in talking with other Christians, an experience like Francis de Sales's seems virtually inevitable in the life of most Christians. The only thing unusual about Francis's experience is that it was so short. What usually happens is that we enter a period of dryness occupied with legalism and scruples, and leave it moved by grace and love. Before, we were quick to condemn; now we are quick to intercede. The previous chapter explored many difficulties in the Christian life, but this chapter will focus on the internal spiritual challenge known as the "dark night of the soul," or a desert experience.

The Beginning

At the beginning of the spiritual journey, the new believer seeks nothing more than to be in church, in prayer, or in

[1] Bregy, *The Story of Saint Francis de Sales,* 18–19.

Scripture, for nothing else brings such great pleasure. This euphoria stage is part of growing up spiritually and should be respected. However, like Francis we may soon find that from the exhilaration of exciting worship, prayer, and evangelism we will be plunged into months or years of spiritual lethargy, boredom, frustration, and confusion.

The wise spiritual adviser will eventually need to tell the new believer, ever so gently, that maturity will one day demand that the euphoric feelings on which he or she is becoming dependent must come to an end. Feelings, even spiritual feelings, can become a roadblock to further spiritual growth; sooner or later, God in His mercy will begin the weaning process to mature the believer's faith.

Few writers understood this spiritual need as clearly as did John of the Cross, who coined the famous phrase, "dark night of the soul." John noted that shortly after conversion, God often "nurtures and caresses the soul . . . like a loving mother who warms her child with the heat of her bosom, nurses it with good milk and tender food, and carries and caresses it in her arms."[2] The new believer, says John, finds his or her joy in spending lengthy periods in prayer, "perhaps even entire nights." Even fasts provoke happiness, and the sacraments bring a special joy.

The ecstasies of life in Christ have been widely understood and documented. The author of *The Cloud of Unknowing* wrote, "God . . . will give man his reward in bliss both in body and in soul. In giving that reward, he sometimes inflames the body of his devout servants with wonderful pleasures here in this life, not only once or twice, but very often in some

[2]John of the Cross, "The Dark Night," in *Selected Writings*, I:1:2.

cases as he may wish. . . . Such pleasures are not to be held suspect."[3]

Fénelon pointed out that "this witness by sensation is the support of beginners. It is the milk of tender new-born souls. They have to suck a long time. It would be dangerous to wean them."[4]

According to Francis de Sales, these "foretastes of heavenly delight" are used by God to withdraw us from "earthly pleasures" and encourage us in the "pursuit of divine love."[5]

As unregenerate people, we operate out of the sensual, so God uses the senses to draw us to Him. In time, however, He will withdraw the sensual support and the weaning process will begin.

Why God Steps Back

"Spiritual caressing," if left unabated, would eventually cause us to lose focus. Thus we could begin to enjoy the fruits of worshiping God (our feelings) more than we enjoyed the God we worship. Augustine wrote, "Whosoever seeketh of God anything besides God, doth not love God purely. If a wife loved her husband, because he is rich, she is not pure, for she loveth not her husband, but the gold of her husband."[6]

Another danger of ongoing spiritual euphoria is that we

[3]Anonymous, *The Cloud of Unknowing*, XLVIII:2.

[4]Fénelon, *Christian Perfection*, 48. The ancients understood that God can easily "outpleasure" the world and Satan and that, under His sovereign direction, this can be a powerful antidote for sin. Cf. à Kempis: "Spiritual comforts exceed all the delights of the world and the pleasures of the flesh" (II:10:1).

[5]de Sales, *Introduction to a Devout Life*, 331.

[6]Augustine, *Sermon 137*, cited in *Confessions*, 46. See also Augustine's words in *Psalm 72*, section 32, cited in *Confessions*, 46: "Whoso seeks from God any other reward but God, and for it would serve God, esteems what he wishes to receive, more than Him from whom he would receive it. What then? Hath God no reward? None, save Himself. The reward of God is God Himself."

become spiritually proud. John of the Cross warned that a "certain kind of secret pride is generated" in us when the feelings remain intense. We "develop a desire somewhat vain—at times very vain—to speak of spiritual things in others' presence, and sometimes even to instruct rather than be instructed." Some of us can become so "evil-minded" that we do not want anyone except ourselves to appear holy, and so by both word and deed we "condemn and detract others whenever the occasion arises."[7]

Most pastors are familiar with this pride, which rises and grips baby believers within their churches. The beginner, having been a Christian for a relatively short time, thinks he or she could pastor better than the pastor, lead better than the elders, teach better than any of the teachers, and direct worship better than the worship leader.

In addition to pride, spiritual gluttony can lead to a deep anger once the delight and satisfaction of spiritual worship pass. We feel angry at God for "leaving" us or angry at ourselves for losing the feelings or angry at the worship leader or pastor we believe is blocking the sensual satisfaction.

If we do not become impatient with others, we may become impatient with ourselves, and thus reveal our pride. We mistakenly believed that the spiritual feelings were a reward for our exceptional spiritual commitment, so we now mistakenly believe that by somehow increasing our spiritual heroics we can bring the feelings back. John of the Cross said we need patience to humbly wait for God to do His work in our souls, but we, addicted to spiritual highs, refuse to wait for God and try to push through the desert with a desperate thrust of the will.

---

[7]John of the Cross, "The Dark Night," in *Selected Writings*, I:2:1–2.

Unwise counselors may try to tell us we should fight the loss of feelings. Yet gluttony for spiritual feelings opens a wide door to the other appetites, including greed, overeating, sexual lusts, the hunger for power, and other sins. When feelings become the focus of our faith, religion becomes not a friend but an enemy, concealing the true state of our heart. We wonder why we fall into sin so soon after a seemingly powerful encounter with God. What we fail to realize is that our hearts were stolen by spiritual gluttony, not real reverence. We have been misled into believing that these feelings are an indication of the temperature of our hearts and the commitment of our will. They are not.

So God steps back. He stubbornly denies us the spiritual feelings with which we've grown so familiar. This is frequently accompanied by very dry periods, times when our prayers seem to bounce off the ceiling and our hearts feel like hot, dry sand. God does this so He can irrigate our desert with the cold water of pure faith, so He can break our addiction to the sensual and call us to the truly spiritual, and so we can humbly say, without doubt or need for reinforcement, "O God, You are my God, and I will follow You all of my days."

Man-Made Deserts

Although the coming and going of the desert experience is largely an act of God's sovereign care for us, spiritual dryness in general can have many causes, including some we create ourselves. For instance, according to Francis de Sales, it is possible to bring on something like a dark night by over-exerting our bodies in an attempt at heroic spiritual growth. "It sometimes happens that spiritual dryness proceeds from an indisposition of body, as when, through an excess of watching, labor, or fasting, we find ourselves oppressed by fatigue, drowsiness, lassitude, and the like infirmities, which, though they depend on the body, yet are calculated to incommode the spirit also, on account of the intimate connection that subsists between both. . . . So St. Francis [Assisi] ordained that his religious should use such moderation in their labors as not to oppress the fervor of their spirits."[8]

De Sales went on to give six additional reasons for the onset of dryness. The first reason is the classical teaching on God's breaking us of spiritual gluttony. "As a mother refuses to gratify the appetite of her child, when such gratification might increase its indisposition, so God withholds consolations from us, when we take a vain complacency in them, and are subject to the spiritual maladies of self-conceit and presumption."

Second, Francis warned that when we neglect to "gather the sweetness and delights of the love of God at the proper season," then God will remove the feelings from us "in punishment of our sloth." The third reason is that we can become overly pleased "in the bed of sensual consolations," and God needs to wean us. The fourth reason is that if we are not honest with our spiritual director, if we mislead him or her with half-lies and deceits, God will send dryness to call us into truth. A fifth reason is that we have immersed ourselves in worldly pleasures and therefore are unable to enjoy "spiritual delights" because they are distasteful to us.

Finally, if we have been careful to preserve the fruits of the consolations we have already received, we can expect to receive new ones. But if we have carelessly lost what was given us, we will not receive any more.[9]

[8]de Sales, *Introduction to a Devout Life*, 332–33.
[9]Ibid., 323–24.

To come out of spiritual dryness, Francis urged that we examine whether any of these six reasons apply, but "this examination is not to be made either with inquietude or too much curiosity." If we can't find a reason for our lack of spiritual feelings, we shouldn't trouble ourselves, but "with all simplicity": (1) Humble ourselves before God, acknowledging our own "nothingness and misery"; (2) Call upon God and beg comfort of him; and (3) Go to our confessor, and "opening to him the several plaits and folds" of our soul, "follow his advice with the utmost simplicity and humility."

But if, after all this, we are still in a state of dryness, we should remember that "there is nothing so profitable, so fruitful, in a state of spiritual dryness, as not to suffer our affections to be too strongly fixed upon the desire of being delivered from it. I do not say that we ought not simply to wish for a deliverance, but that we should not set our heart upon it. . . . In the midst of our spiritual dryness, let us never lose courage, but wait with patience for return of consolation."[10]

Feelings Forecast

The wisdom of the ancients teaches us that spiritual feelings should be looked at like today's weather forecast. The weather can make our work more pleasant or more difficult, but it should never define our task. Likewise, feelings may make our spiritual lives easier or harder, but those feelings should never direct our spiritual lives.

At times we'll be virtually singing as our prayers flow from a heart full of God's joy. At other times each word will come

[10]Ibid., 324–26.

forth only after the most severe labor. Feelings will make prayer and devotion seem easier or harder, but that's about all the thought we should give to them. The author of *The Cloud of Unknowing* exhorted readers, "Toward . . . sweetness and pleasures, physical or spiritual, no matter how pleasing nor how holy they may be, we should have an attitude of unconcern. If they come, welcome them; but do not depend on them lest it weaken you, for it will take up a great deal of your strength if you remain with these sweet pleasures for a long time."[11]

Just as an overly pleasant day, weatherwise, can distract us from our work, so an overly pleasant sensual experience in devotion can distract us from truly offering up our wills to God. We must avoid the trap of equating "good worship" with "good feeling." The two are unrelated. De Sales noted, "Devotion does not always consist in that sweetness, delight, consolation, or sensible tenderness of heart, which moves us to tears, and causes us to find satisfaction in some spiritual exercises."[12]

In fact, as we've already learned, spiritual feelings can actually be our enemies if they mislead us to believe something that is false or cause us to overestimate our maturity or level of commitment. Not only can they lead us into false teaching, but they can also mislead us into believing we have some "secret knowledge" or "special relationship" with God that exalts us above the rest.

We must learn to live God-directed lives; feelings are never the yardstick of truth. They will betray the truth far more often than they will confirm it.

[11]Anonymous, *The Cloud of Unknowing*, L:1.
[12]de Sales, *Introduction to a Devout Life*, 315.

The Journey of the Dark Night

The dark night of the soul can come in many different forms and in varying degrees. It can be a cyclical experience, returning as God ordains, or go on for days, months, or years without abating. We all have different needs and different attitudes and addictions that need to be burned up within us. When we don't understand what is happening or when we're told that a loss of religious feeling is evidence that we've turned from our first love, the dark night may make us angry at God. Fortunately, God does not fear our anger, and the dark night will come in spite of it. Keeping some of the wisdom of the ancients in mind will help us as we journey through the dark night.

1. Respect the Necessity of Silence

One of the hardest things I've ever done is hold my then-three-year-old son's hand and look into his eyes while a doctor put stitches in his forehead. Graham couldn't believe I would let someone hurt him so much, and his eyes pierced my heart as he pleaded with me to let him go.

Now imagine if someone were whispering into my son's ear, "If your father really loved you, he wouldn't let this man do this to you. If you were my son, I wouldn't abandon you this way."

Satan often does this during a dark night. God is leading us through a hard but necessary journey—and silence is a vital aspect of this journey—but Satan will tempt us to believe God is being cruel or that God is abandoning us or that we have somehow pushed God away or "lost" the Holy Spirit or any number of lies. The truth is, God is simply calling us into maturity. He is preparing us to drive "blind," without sensual support, through the night of faith.

His silence, then, is not abandonment or agreement with the accuser's twisted logic. It is a necessary weaning of sensual support.

2. Remember That You Are Not Alone

When we begin to sense we are entering a dry spell, we need to know, as Thomas à Kempis pointed out, that this is how God has always treated His saints. "If great saints were so dealt with, we that are weak and poor ought not to despair, if we be sometimes fervent and sometimes cold; for the Spirit cometh and goeth, according to the good pleasure of his own will. . . . I never found any so religious and devout, that he had not sometimes a withdrawing of grace, or felt not some decrease of zeal. There was never saint so highly rapt and illuminated, who first or last was not tempted. For he is not worthy of the high contemplation of God, who hath not been exercised with some tribulation for God's sake."[13]

The barrenness of these spiritual deserts can be excruciating. When we face them it will be an encouragement for us to realize that others, in fact most Christians, have experienced, to one degree or another, what we are experiencing. We are not abnormal or less committed Christians for going through this dry spell. We do not need to uncover buried sins that are stealing our joy. We are simply average Christians going through a normal spiritual process.

The confessions of other Christians who have faced spiritual barrenness can encourage us and remind us we are not alone. Consider the emptiness described by Francis de Sales:

[13] à Kempis, *The Imitation of Christ*, II:9:5, 7.

"Sometimes you shall find yourself so absolutely destitute of all feeling of devotion that your soul shall seem to be a wild, fruitless, barren desert, in which there is no trace of a pathway to find her God, nor any water of grace to refresh her, on account of the dryness which seems to threaten her with a total and absolute desolation."[14]

3. Remember That God Is Not Judging You for Having Less Feeling

Spiritual feelings are not a gauge of our maturity, and God will not judge us when the spiritual feelings wane. Thomas à Kempis urged that we not lose heart when the feelings fly. "All therefore is not lost, if sometimes thou hast less feeling for Me . . . than thou wouldest. That good and sweet affection which thou sometimes feelest, is the effect of grace present, and a sort of foretaste of thy heavenly home; but hereon thou must not lean too much, for it comes and goes."[15]

Don't let self-accusation create a wall between you and God; the feelings weren't a reward, and their withdrawal is not a punishment.

4. Remember That Feelings Have a Limited Role in Christian Living

Some Christians grow so dependent on spiritual pampering, they would prefer to remain comfortable in their immaturity than to press on to true faith. When God takes the feelings away, we need to remember that spiritual feelings are the beginning, not the end, of Christian living. Fénelon wrote, "How many souls, having had too tender a childhood in Jesus

[14]de Sales, *Introduction to a Devout Life*, 322.
[15]à Kempis, *The Imitation of Christ*, III:6:2.

Christ, too delicate, too dependent on so mild a milk, draw back and give up the life within, when God begins to wean them! . . . They make the sanctuary of what was only the porch of the temple."[16]

5. Take Up Your Cross

Fénelon urged that we follow God as He steps back and thus step back from ourselves. Dying to self, after all, is one of the primary purposes of this weaning. "We never so need to abandon ourselves to God as when he seems to abandon us. So let us take light and consolations when he gives them, but without becoming attached to them. When he plunges us into the night of pure faith, then let us go into this night, and let us lovingly suffer this agony. One moment is worth a thousand in this tribulation."[17]

When we love Christ only for what He brings us, including spiritual feelings, we are loving ourselves, not loving Him, regardless of the sacrifice we think we are offering. The dark night of the soul purifies our motivation and keeps us from becoming like the crowds in the New Testament who followed Jesus, not for His teaching, but for the miraculously supplied bread.[18]

Rather than fight the withdrawal of spiritual feelings, then, we should let them call us to the cross. God's "tough love" is far more stubborn and enduring than our petty rebellion anyway. Instead of anger or rebellion, our attitudes should reflect humility. We never deserved the spiritual feelings in the first place, so we can hardly claim them as our right when

[16]Fénelon, *Christian Perfection*, 152.
[17]Ibid., 56.
[18]See Fénelon, *Christian Perfection*, 151.

they are taken away.[19] Teresa of Avila gently but firmly cuts us to our knees by pointing out, "It's an amusing thing that even though we still have a thousand impediments and imperfections and our virtues have hardly begun to grow . . . we are yet not ashamed to seek spiritual delights in prayer or to complain about dryness."[20]

One of the great temptations during the desert is to arrogantly demand that God end the dryness at once. We remind God how much we have left for Him when in reality we should be praising Him for how much He delivered us from; we remind God how zealously we have served Him when in reality we should be thanking Him for giving us purpose. We live with a distorted view of our own spirituality. If we do not embrace humility—if we do not go to the cross—we will very likely embrace anger and instead of maturing in our walk with Christ, we will be stuck in a spiritual cul-de-sac.

6. Don't Seek Spiritual Feeling in New Circumstances

When we first begin to notice the sensory delights slipping away, the worst thing we can do is run to find them through some new spiritual experience. Not only can that lead to a counterfeit faith, but even at best it simply works against what God is doing within our souls.

The temptation to flight can be great. Like a man or woman mad with thirst, we can run circles in the desert and willingly drink water from a radiator if it will wet our throats. John of

[19]"O Lord, I am not worthy of thy consolation, nor of any spiritual visitation; and therefore thou dealest justly with me, when thou leavest me poor and desolate. For though I could shed a sea of tears, yet should I not be worthy of thy consolation" (à Kempis, *Imitation of Christ*, III:52:1).

[20]Teresa of Avila, *The Interior Castle*, II:1:7.

the Cross warned of those who refuse to accept God's with-drawal of the delight: "All their time is spent looking for satis-faction and spiritual consolation; they can never read enough spiritual books, and one minute they are meditating on one subject and the next on another, always in search for some gratification in the things of God. God very rightly and dis-creetly and lovingly denies this satisfaction to these begin-ners. If He did not, they would fall into innumerable evils because of their spiritual gluttony and craving for sweetness. Wherefore it is important for these beginners to enter the dark night and be purged of this childishness."[21]

Fénelon advised Christians to "remain serene in the trial, and not torment [yourself] by dwelling on what God is taking away from [you]."[22] How sad it is when Christians seek out one church after another and attend one camp meeting or convention after another in a desperate search for the delight God is purposefully holding back. Such people are particularly vulnerable to new teachers who seem exciting and who prom-ise the experience they so desperately seek—and there is no shortage of teachers who will gladly reinforce this "exciting" element to build the transfer membership of their church or television ministry.

7. Surrender

For those who have found themselves in a desert and con-tinue to argue with God about it, I urge you to surrender. I've never seen anybody win. God has more patience than we have rebellion. It is often only when we submit and learn what He wants us to learn that He will bring us out, but even

[21]John of the Cross, "The Dark Night," in *Selected Writings*, I:6:6.
[22]Fénelon, *Christian Perfection*, 48.

this is a dangerous statement. If we submit only to be relieved of our desert, we're not learning our lesson—we're simply bargaining.

The dark night is a fearsome journey, but once traveled it produces a new depth of intimacy worth every bit of satisfaction that the dark night took away. The darker the night, as the saying goes, the brighter the dawn. We will talk about this new depth in a moment. Before we do this, however, we need to consider a certain type of Christian that is particularly vulnerable to spiritual feelings and therefore may feel the dark night even more acutely than most—the sensual Christian.

Sensual Christians

Before, we talked about spiritual feelings as being a stage in the Christian life, but the rising and falling of spiritual feelings can also be related to our spiritual temperaments. Some of us are primarily motivated by intellectualism, others by activism, and still others by sensual stimulation. Those in this latter group are likely to have ongoing and more intense struggles with spiritual gluttony. We are most vulnerable to whatever feeds us, and some of us, by temperament, are fed more by sensual feelings than others. We can even become addicted to the feelings and thus think we need them. When they are withdrawn, we immediately lapse into sin. *In The Cloud of Unknowing,* we read:

> Some persons are so weak and tender of spirit that if they were not comforted by some feelings of pleasure they would not be able to bear the diversity of temptations and troubles that they encounter at the hands of their physical and spiritual enemies in this life. . . . On the other hand, there are some persons

who are so strong in spirit that they can derive sufficient pleasure for themselves within their own souls by offering this reverent and meek stirring of love and their will in accord with God. They do not need to be sustained by pleasures in their bodily feelings.[23]

God treats His children as individuals. There is no single time line all Christians must follow, and there is no single spiritual temperament. God treats us according to how He created us. This should cause us to respect the differing needs of Christians for spiritual feelings. Fénelon wrote, "The invalid who cannot walk without a cane cannot let anyone take it away from him. He feels his weakness. He fears to fall, and he is right. But he ought not to be upset to see a healthy and strong man who does not need the same support. The healthy man walks more freely without a cane. But he should never be contemptuous of him who cannot do without it."[24]

In other words, if we are discipling or directing others, we shouldn't look down upon those who need spiritual feelings to fight sin. On the other hand, those who have a very sensual faith shouldn't look down upon those who seem to have a "boring" faith in comparison with their own.

A New Depth

Once we've passed through the purgation (and this is often a cyclical process), we experience a new depth in which we live by faith, not feeling. The author of *The Cloud of Unknowing* wrote, "I would hope to lead you away from the boister-

[23]Anonymous, *The Cloud of Unknowing,* L:3.
[24]Fénelon, *Christian Perfection,* 141.

ousness of physical feeling and toward the purity and depth of spiritual feeling." He continued, "When our desires have physical qualities mingled with them, as they do when we stress and strain ourselves in spirit and body together, we are then further from God than we would be if we proceeded more devoutly and soberly in purity and depth of spirit." He concluded, "the greater the spiritual quality of your soul, the less is its physical quality."[25]

When we live by faith and not by feelings, when we persevere no matter how dry we feel, Teresa of Avila said, we show we are among those souls who "would want the Lord to see that they do not serve Him for pay."[26] That is, we want the Lord to see that we will serve Him regardless of whether it gives us pleasure or pain. We will serve Him because He is God and Lord and because He has captured our hearts and our wills. "The desires these souls have are no longer for consolations or spiritual delight, since the Lord Himself is present with these souls and it is His Majesty who now lives."[27]

Having passed through the desert, we are not so easily shaken. Strong feelings no longer move us. We may still enjoy them, but they do not overwhelm us; they do not direct us. We have learned to submit our will to God, to be moved by truth and His Spirit. Spiritual feelings are no longer our Seeing Eye dogs but rather little Chihuahuas dancing at our feet.

Reflections

Read Matthew 28:27–50. Was Christ's work on the cross pleasing to God? Read Psalm 22. How do you think Christ

[25]Anonymous, *The Cloud of Unknowing*, XLVII:2–4.
[26]Teresa of Avila, *The Interior Castle*, VI:9:18.
[27]Ibid., VII:3:8.

felt during the crucifixion? Did this have anything to do with His obedience, faith, commitment, or maturity?

When have you felt farthest from God? Were you, in fact, far from God, or were your feelings just absent?

When have you felt closest to God? Do you believe you really were closest to God at this point, or were your feelings deceiving you?

Chapter Eleven

Seasons of the Soul:
The Passages of the Spiritual Life

> *Ecclesiastes declares that there is a time for everything under heaven, and everything may be taken to refer to our spiritual life. If this is so, then we ought to examine the matter; and we should do everything in proper season.* John Climacus

Blaise Pascal possessed one of the greatest mathematical minds of his day. Many people, in fact, know him more for his contributions to math and science than for his Christian devotion. Pascal's father had planned to guide Blaise through language studies before introducing him to mathematics, but that stopped the day he found Blaise working on his own, playing with figures drawn on the floor. When he asked Blaise what he was doing, Blaise answered that he was trying to express the relationship between the angles of a triangle and two right angles. In other words, Blaise was working on the thirty-second proposition in Book 1 of Euclid's *Elements of Geometry*.

By the time he was twenty, Pascal had gained national notoriety by creating a math machine that performed the four basic functions of arithmetic. He later became famous for his work in physics.

But near the end of his short life, Pascal wrote in a letter that while the study of geometry is a valuable way of learning to reason correctly and the highest exercise of the mind, it is only a métier, or trade, and ultimately useless.[1] Pascal had found something to study that was even more difficult than math: humankind.

Pascal wrote in *Pensées*, "fewer people study man than mathematics. It is only because they do not know how to study man that people look into all the rest."[2] *Pensées*, perhaps more than any other classic, studies the nature of men and women. In this study, Pascal came up with several provocative thoughts: "If we are too young our judgment is impaired," he wrote, "just as it is if we are too old."[3] Or this: "Man is so made that if he is told often enough that he is a fool he believes it. By telling himself so often enough he convinces himself, because when he is alone he carries on an inner dialogue with himself which is important to keep under proper control."[4]

Taking our cue from Pascal, we will use this chapter to explore what it means to be a man or a woman on a spiritual journey. Like Pascal, we want to explore what it is that moves us and what it is that makes the spiritual life difficult and exciting. Fortunately, as we look back, we have much help.

One of my first delights after my initial forays into the spiritual classics was the realization that these ancient writers understood human nature far more than many of the modern psychologists I had studied in college. As I read more and more, I began to understand that this is what makes the

[1] Hugh Davidson, *Blaise Pascal* (Boston: Twayne Publishers, 1983), 3, 21.
[2] Pascal, *Pensées*, 245.
[3] Ibid., 35.
[4] Ibid., 55.

difference between a book that lasts for hundreds or thousands of years and one that is out of print within months.

The classics are classics because they are rooted in reality. When people read them, they see themselves and know that someone understands. The classics don't speak platitudes of idealism to a community that pretends. On the contrary, they speak the painful truth that nourishes souls who hunger for authenticity.

Studying spiritual growth requires that we understand the human condition—not just its difficulties, for we've discussed that already, but the stages, conditions, and challenges of the Christian life. Those who have gone before us have recognized that the spiritual life has a natural progression of highs and lows, peaks and valleys. I've identified three elements of the Christian life that express this progression—spiritual *terrain, climates,* and *stations.*

Too many Christians suffer from the illusion that there is one spiritual prescription for every Christian, yet the classics are full of the understanding that we all face a different spiritual terrain, climate, and station, and therefore have different needs and capabilities.[5] Furthermore, the spiritual life is such a fluid life that there is not even one program that will fit one person for his or her entire life. Our spiritual climate, terrain, and stations will change, so our spiritual understanding must change as well. Let's look at each of these passages carefully.

Spiritual Climates

Spiritual climates refer to the environments in which we serve God. If we live in a religious community as a monk or

[5]I am also convinced that we each have our own spiritual temperament, but this subject is so large it will be the topic of my next book.

a nun, our climate will be much different from that in a college fraternity or sorority. A woman who lives with a believing and supportive husband exists in a very different climate from a woman who is berated and mocked by a nonbelieving husband. A child growing up in a warm and supportive atmosphere has a different climate from one growing up in a household driven by alcoholism and blatantly immoral behavior.

Some of our climates are chosen, while others are not. Men and women choose, for instance, who they want to marry, and this choice will greatly affect their spiritual climate in the years to come. But a child does not choose what home to be born in. The five main climates in our lives are our home, our work, our social relationships, our church, and our personal climate. Most of us can't choose, or in some cases even improve, every one of our climates. On the other hand, most of us do have at least one or two climates we can change to create a better foundation on which to build the rest of our spiritual lives.

The importance or relevance of a healthy spiritual climate may never have occurred to us, but the concept itself shouldn't be a surprise. People go south all the time to improve their physical health, so why shouldn't Christians consider changing spiritual climates to improve their spiritual health?

Home

A fairly easy question to ask is, Does your home life make your faith easier or harder? Additional questions to ask yourself include: Are you faced with temptation because of your climate more than you are faced with encouragement to grow in holiness? Is prayer made more difficult or easier? If you need someone to talk to about spiritual matters, is someone available? If you need encouragement, can you find it?

By beginning with these questions, you'll soon think of many others. Take the time to evaluate the spiritual climate of your living arrangement. Once you've evaluated it, ask God if there is something you can do to improve it. Or if you see that the climate you are now in is clearly detrimental, can it be changed? You might not be able to move, but can you talk to the people you live with to help create a better environment? Why force yourself to stay in a spiritual winter when you can create a spring?

One caution is in order here, however. Some climates may be difficult because of the ministry we have been called to, so we can't escape them. Because we live in several different climates, however, we can strengthen those climates that need to be strengthened so we can better endure those climates that must be endured. Our home climate is particularly crucial; it is the foundation to every other climate.

Work

If every Christian sought a pleasant work climate, we might be happier Christians, but the world wouldn't be evangelized. And some people must put up with the degrading attitudes and speech of others because they need the paycheck and no other job is available. The way to an improved work climate may not be to flee but to prayerfully transform the place where we work.

I wrote earlier about my experiment with "positive gossip." In prayer, perhaps you can come up with some similarly positive remedies. The key is to try to be an agent of transformation, rather than becoming complacent. If your spiritual life is being depleted and yet the people around you aren't being changed, it may well be that your effectiveness is at an end and you need to seek a new place of employment.

Social Relationships

While evangelism may call us to live and work in unfavorable climates, who we socialize with is our choice and should be made carefully. In fact, the apostle Paul and the writer of Proverbs, among others, expressly urge us to be discerning in our social relationships.[6]

Few Christians can thrive if every climate is adverse, and this climate is relatively easy to change because it is part of our leisure time. Are your friends true friends? Do they encourage you, or do you find yourself continually falling with them into unhealthy practices? Is there someone who invariably leads you to gossip? Is there someone else who always seems negative?

This doesn't necessarily mean we must end such relationships, though in some cases it may mean we should be willing to. In either case, we should aggressively seek out positive relationships that build us and the other person up so that together, we can grow in the faith.

Church

Increasing attention is being paid to "churches that abuse" and congregations that use rather than build up the body of Christ. Are you in a church that supports the role God has called you to, or is the church more concerned with meeting the needs of the institution? Are you in a place where you can exercise the gifts God has given you? Does the church prepare you to interact with the world, or is it keeping you so preoccupied that you have no time to reach out to the world?

[6]See Prov. 22:24; 1 Cor. 5:9–11; and 2 Thess. 3:14.

Does the church create a climate in which your personal growth is inevitable, or are you finding that the church is putting stumbling blocks in your way? Has the church created a warm, caring, and supportive environment, or does it operate on fear, guilt, secrecy, and manipulation?

Personal Self-Talk and Behavior

You can influence this environment more than any other one. What type of climate are you creating for yourself with your self-talk and your daily actions? Remember Pascal's earlier statement—are you continually telling yourself you're a fool, or are you learning how to have a healthy inner dialogue?

I'm learning that as I go through the day I'm bringing either sunshine or rain into my life based on how I talk to myself and others. By evaluating what I'm thinking and saying, I can determine whether I'm encouraging myself or making myself more miserable. Primarily, I want God's perspective because mine is never balanced.

Putting the Climates Together

As a runner who travels around the nation, I've learned to adjust my running according to where I am. It can be quite an experience to run in Virginia, wake up two days later for a jog in Denver, the "mile-high city," and then run a day later in southern California. I can't tell how I'm feeling, really, because there is no consistency of climate. The "scale" is different every time my fitness is measured.

Spiritually, we also face those times when there is no consistency of climate. What amazes me, though, is that many Christians never even consider or evaluate their climates. If times are hard, they're not sure why. It is idealistic to assume that what's going on around us won't affect us; climate matters.

Take the time, then, to evaluate each climate we've discussed. Which is your strongest one? Which is your weakest? Can you improve any of them?

But as you do this exercise, remember that many circumstances are there by God's design, and you need a healthy respect for God's sovereignty. It's not as simple as stating, "This climate is difficult so I'm going to change it." If we've made it difficult, or if we've chosen the difficult climate, it only makes sense to try to change it. But when the climate is there by God's design, we simply must endure.

Climacus wrote, "[God] has often been known to act in the following way: when He sees courageous souls He permits them to be embattled from the very beginning, in order the sooner to reward them."[7]

Olympic athletes often intentionally seek out more difficult climates to get greater benefit from their training. Runners may purposely flock to the higher altitudes of the mountains. When God wants to prepare His sons and daughters for a particular work, He may place them in adverse climates that will test them to the very limit.

In these seasons, I've found it's helpful to remember two things: climates change, and God is aware of my situation. Rain passes and winter eventually turns to spring. Just as importantly, God doesn't expect me to run as fast or as far in a snowstorm as I might run on a beautiful autumn day. Fénelon urged patience. "Wait until the winter is past, and until God has made all die which ought to die, then the spring revives all."[8]

Spiritual climates do not predetermine our spiritual growth,

[7]Climacus, *The Ladder of Divine Ascent*, 78–79.
[8]Fénelon, *Christian Perfection*, 173.

but they do affect it. We have to allow for them. Part of our quest to draw near to God should involve creating supportive climates that will encourage our quest.

Spiritual Terrain

Spiritual terrain refers to the "road" on which we're traveling. We may be in a very supportive environment—a pleasant climate—but going uphill all way.

You can have the most supportive spiritual climate of any person in your church, but if you get laid off from your job, contract a serious disease, have a visa denied that keeps you from fulfilling your dream of becoming a missionary, or lose a loved one to death, your spiritual life is going to be affected.

Spiritual terrain can also refer to the inner realities of your spiritual life—a lack or a preponderance of doubt, a lack of enjoyment or disinterest in prayer, intimacy or distance with God—any of these realities, which seem to come and go, may affect your spiritual growth.

Experienced runners going up a hill don't get discouraged when they move only with great effort. They recognize that, although the pace is slower and requires more effort, the reason lies in the terrain, not in how well they are doing. If these runners crest the hill and begin going down, they don't assume they are feeling better simply because they now run faster with less effort; on the contrary, they recognize that the terrain has again changed. When we don't take the spiritual terrain into account, we may be doing better or worse than we think; our walk with Christ may feel like a struggle, but that's only because of the difficulties we're going through.

After a speaking engagement in New Hampshire, I had an afternoon to myself and drove north to hike in the White

Mountains. After hiking for quite some time, I wasn't sure if I would be able to make it to the top by nightfall, and since I was unfamiliar with the trail I asked a couple of hikers coming down how much farther I had to go. They had left the top an hour earlier, one of them said, but the trail was very steep and I'd be very foolish to assume that because they could travel down in an hour, I could travel up in an hour.

In the same way, we can't make direct comparisons between our experiences and the experiences of others because we all face different spiritual terrains.

When faced with a difficult terrain, we need to remember that just as seasons change, so trails level out. On the other hand, those who are having it particularly easy should remember that around the corner the trail may lead uphill. Ignatius urged those fighting "desolation" or difficulty to remember that they will one day be in a state of "consolation" and ease. He urged those in the joyous state of consolation to remember that one day they will be back in desolation.[9]

The point is that we can't expect the same from ourselves when we are going uphill as when we are going downhill. God doesn't, and a wise spiritual counselor won't either. Just because we seem to be struggling more doesn't necessarily mean there is a hidden sin or that we have lost our faith or that we have grown lukewarm; it could simply mean we are traveling uphill, and until the terrain flattens out, we're going to be going forward with great effort.

Stations in Life

Our stations in life are the roles we must play as husbands and wives, sons and daughters, fathers and mothers, brothers

[9]Ignatius Loyola, *Spiritual Exercises*, 109.

and sisters, hired or retired, single or widowed. The fascinating thing about stations is that they change. A sixteen-year-old and a sixty-year-old have different roles to play in society; they also have different roles to play in the church, and their spirituality will be different as well.

It's very likely that some of the people reading this book may have grown frustrated and even discouraged as they encountered the challenges of John Climacus, William Law, Thomas à Kempis, and the others. They may feel these saints are so far above them in their spiritual lives they fall into despair and are tempted to just give up instead of being encouraged or inspired.

Understanding the stations of the spiritual life is crucial to maintain a proper perspective. A young mother with three children under the age of six cannot expect to have the same spiritual opportunities as Teresa of Avila, who lived as a celibate woman and who wrote *The Interior Castle* in her later years after decades of walking in close communion with Christ. A married, working man with children cannot expect to enter into the full reality spoken of by John of the Cross, a member of a religious order who was not married and had no children. If we try to leap stations, we won't glorify God; we will just frustrate ourselves.

Even William Law, who called for a very demanding spirituality, understood the need to tailor our spirituality to our station in life. "Those who have most leisure seem more especially called to a more eminent observance of these holy rules of a devout life. And they who by the necessity of their state and not through their own choice have but little time to employ thus must make the best use of that little they have."[10]

[10]Law, *A Serious Call*, 208.

The spiritual program for a woman working sixty hours a week as a stockbroker is going to be much different from one for a college student taking twelve credits and going home on the weekends. Each individual has his or her own particular temptations and challenges.

According to Francis de Sales, even our sins should be evaluated in light of our station.[11] "Young beginners in devotion . . . commit certain faults. . . . That low and servile fear which begets excessive scruples in the souls of new converts from a course of sin, is commendable in beginners, and a certain foreboding of a future purity of conscience; but the same fear would be blamable in those who are far advanced, in whose heart love ought to reign, which by imperceptible degrees chases away this kind of servile fear."[12]

Excessive scruples is actually a fairly common stage after a new believer's conversion or rededication—not only in the lives of those who had much to repent of, such as an Ignatius or Augustine, but also in the lives of people such as Francis de Sales, who lived a relatively "clean" life and would not appear to be naturally subject to such a tortured conscience. Maturity, however, led each of these men to a deeper faith based on love rather than guilt.

"Excessive scruples" is one thing in a new believer, but quite another in one who should have matured and left this "spiritual hypochondria" behind. People wonder why God seemed so angry at some biblical leaders and punished them for what appeared to be rather minor sins—such as when God told Moses to hit the rock in a certain way to bring forth

[11]Sin is always sin, of course, but what we're talking about is finding the best remedy for sin. A single person, for example, will have a different struggle with lust than a married person. The sin may be the same, but the prescription won't be.

[12]de Sales, *Introduction to a Devout Life*, 123.

water for the people of Israel and Moses somehow messed it up and was told he could not enter the promised land (see Deut. 20:1ff.). We have to remember that God expects more from some people than from others. Moses was a key player in salvation history, and God had to keep him on a short leash, so to speak. (Remember, also, that Moses has been and will be rewarded accordingly.) God is not a respecter of persons, but He is, I believe, a respecter of stations.

This is why it is so foolish to wonder why some Christians seem to get away with certain things while others pay dearly for their disobedience. God treats us as individuals. And remember, God is not under the law, He *is* the law.

Stations not only govern how God views us but how we view temptation. At certain stages in our lives, we are more vulnerable to some appetites that lead to various temptations. Augustine talked about this when he separated the temptations he faced as a young man and as the mature man who wrote *Confessions*. As an elder churchman, Augustine was able to remove himself from most sexual temptation by abstaining from all sexual activity. He grew beyond the daily battle with sexual lust that he faced as a young man. However, this was replaced by the temptation of gluttony. Augustine realized he could not escape this temptation, only manage it. He had to eat, and therefore the temptation to abuse food was ever present.

A young couple involved in the business of raising a family will face many temptations. They have to work and earn money, and this necessarily cramps their schedules. Prayer, Bible study, meditation, and fellowship must somehow fit into a day that already has the best hours spoken for. Having a family involves affection for each other and for children, both of which can become obsessive and idolatrous.

An older couple with grown children have temptations of their own. For the first time in their lives, they may have significant disposable income. It was easy to be frugal and responsible when every penny had to be accounted for, but now that there is an abundance, will materialism steal their hearts?

On and on we could go, but the point is clear that different stations in life lead us into different danger zones. We'll eventually grow out of some of these zones, but usually that just means we'll grow into new ones.

The apostle Paul spoke of the many different stages, especially as they relate to age groups.[13] Paul expected different things from different groups. In New Testament times, "elder" was more than a title. The early church used a chronological word, such as elder, to signify an official office because it properly assumed that the office would be filled by those who were not young. There were occasional exceptions, but the general rule was that the office of an elder would be filled by a Christian who had walked through a good part of the Christian life, had grappled with its difficulties, had overcome the basic appetites of particular stations, and could now give guidance in hindsight.

If an elder is struggling through life, or even burdened down with life, be that a young family, a job that requires extra hours, or children that demand extra attention, he is not free to minister to the church. So stations have practical, ecclesiastical significance as well as individual spiritual significance.

Accepting Your Station

I once received a call from a man whose first child was less than a week old. He was bemoaning the virtual eclipse of his

[13]1 Tim. 5:1–3, 9–15; 2 Tim. 2:22; Titus 2:2–8; see also 1 John 2:12–14 for another apostle's view.

spiritual life in the days since the baby had arrived. He hadn't been able to start reading a book I had sent him, and his prayer and Bible study time had suffered.

He was wrestling with the reality of his present station in life, not a rebellious heart. He didn't need guilt; he simply needed perspective. For a season, our prayer time may be cut or we may be forced to develop newer, creative ways of praying. We do this, however, looking forward to a future station in life when we will have more time. If our hearts are right, we can expect a time when the financial need will be less and our work can be curtailed, when the sex drive begins to wane and we may even be able to contemplate celibacy, the "gift that nobody wants." A young married man is playing games if he tries to live like a monk, but there may very well be an opportunity later in life. This doesn't mean we excuse sloppy spiritual living by saying, "I'll get serious later on." Such a statement is born out of complacency and presumption, not wisdom.

From Paul's teaching, we know that God respects the stations. Paul wrote in 1 Corinthians 7:33, "he who is married cares about the things of the world—how he may please his wife" (NKJV). This being so, should we get "unmarried" and therefore undistracted? Paul said no. "Each one should retain the place in life that the Lord assigned to him and to which God has called him" (1 Cor. 7:17 NIV).

If men or women ignore their responsibilities in life with the excuse that they want to live "spiritually" they are mocking God, not serving Him. True spirituality has practical ramifications. It is spiritual to provide for your family (see 1 Tim. 5:8). It is spiritual, even, to express physical intimacy in marriage (see 1 Cor. 7:3ff. and Heb. 13:4).

We need an honest, realistic, and objective view of our

lives, lives of seasons and stations. We can enjoy the young children. We can enjoy without guilt the thrill of working hard at a new vocation. We can deeply appreciate the physical intimacy of marriage. We can slow down a little in retirement. A truly Christian spirituality will incorporate, not fight, these stations; yet all of them must be held loosely, for all of them are transient. Our relationship with God will remain; each of the stations will pass.

Francis de Sales was a master spiritual director, so people often confided in him. One woman, Madame Brulart, desperately sought after the "Christian perfection" being talked about in her day, but Francis gently reminded her that perfections "vary according to the diversity of vocations." Francis further warned Madame Brulart not to alienate her husband or her family due to excessive devotions. "Not only should you be devout yourself and love piety," he wrote, "but you should make it lovable to others."[14]

Another woman, Jeanne Chantal, longed to become a nun so she could devote herself entirely to her faith. Francis was gentle but firm with her, finally saying, "Nothing so impedes our progress in perfection as to be sighing after another way of life."[15]

The heart in tune with the Spirit of God will always find room to seek and know God. Our station in life should not become an excuse to ignore God, but a reality we must live with as we relate to God. We ignore it at our peril.

[14]Bregy, *The Story of Saint Francis de Sales*, 61. I'm convinced that Francis was able to counsel from his own experience on this one. As a young man studying law at the University of Padua, Francis's ascetic habits were often resented by wilder students. Although the provost praised Francis upon his graduation ("You have lived in the midst of a voluptuous city and preserved your innocence"), Francis understood that we can win the war of personal holiness and lose the war of evangelism if we don't respect our surroundings.

[15]Ibid., 62.

The Temptation of the Teacher

We can wreck sincere hearts if we don't allow for spiritual climates, terrains, or stations. We do this by asking something that someone is not capable of giving or wanting someone to advance too quickly, or allowing him or her to proceed too slowly. Those Christians who seek a ministry of healing and counsel and who want to participate in soul surgery must therefore take great care to broaden their experience by listening to others. Soul surgery would be so easy if there were one prescription for every sin, but spiritual reality is not as simple as that. A medical student has the advantage of having to master just two bodies—male and female. Spiritual problems tend to be much more complex and varied, and spiritual counselors can do more harm than good if they fail to appreciate the spiritual diversity of the multifaceted body of Christ.

The temptation to teach others when we are on a spiritual "high" is great—but dangerous. We often have an idealized view when we feel so well, and we run the danger of disillusioning other Christians by speaking as if we floated on this earth rather than walked. On the other hand, if we are facing particularly difficult struggles, we may mistakenly assume that every Christian struggles in this way and we may be tempted to speak only of the difficulty of the Christian life.

Do you see the great danger here? If we do not recognize the objective valleys and hills, the summers and winters, we run a great risk of subjectifying the faith—interpreting everyone's faith by our own particular and seasonal experiences. Our teaching and preaching will always be out of balance as we struggle from one season to the next.

This is why it can be so dangerous for young Christians to teach. Until we have walked over several hills and through many valleys and begin to understand what the Christian journey entails on a broad time line, we are liable to lose perspective and balance in our teaching. We will imprison our hearers in our experience rather than launch them into the experience that God has for them.

The author of *The Cloud of Unknowing* warned against this tendency when he wrote, "Those who are able to see or experience the perfection of this work only after a long labor and then but seldom may easily be deceived if they speak, think, or judge other men in terms of their own experience, thinking that other men are like them able to achieve it only rarely, and then not without great labor."[16]

Some people may find prayer easier than we do; others may find it much more difficult. Some may drop sin at will and never look back; others may have to slowly grow out of sin's habits. The wise teacher will remember that his or her experience is one story among millions; let's not force every other Christian into our own custom-made box.

God is enthroned in heaven, above all the changing climates; He roams over the earth, above all terrain. He is eternal, above all stations in life. Our confidence should therefore be based on the finished work of Christ. Our strength is based on the limitless power of the Spirit; our favor is based on the mercy and grace of the Father.

If we base the success of our faith on ourselves, we will be disillusioned in the winter and unduly smug in the summer. Even though we are called to cooperate with God's work in our lives, our spiritual existence rests securely in the work of our triune God.

Changing spiritual climates, terrains, and stations cry out

[16]Anonymous, *The Cloud of Unknowing*, LXXII:1.

for an unmovable foundation. If we listen carefully to this cry of our hearts, we will find it is answered by God, and God alone. We will not always be active parents; we will not always be working in a vocation; but we will always be walking with the God who made us, the rock of our faith, the anchor of our soul.

Reflections

What's your spiritual climate? Go through the five climates described in this chapter and evaluate the challenges you must face as you seek to grow. Do you feel like you're in a desert? Read Psalm 78:17–19. What's your greatest temptation in the desert? Read Isaiah 32:1–2. How can you encourage someone in a desert?

What is making your spiritual terrain particularly difficult? Is this difficulty by your choice or God's design? If it's by your choice, what can you do to change it? If it's by God's design, how will the discussion of God as our rock help you to endure? (If your terrain seems very easy, are you preparing for when it may go uphill?)

How would you describe your station in life? What can you reasonably expect from yourself in light of your station? Have you been too hard on yourself, or too easy?

Chapter Twelve

Soul Surgery: A Guide to Spiritual Direction

> *Consult with him that is wise and conscientious and seek to be instructed by a better than thyself, rather than to follow thine own inventions.* Thomas à Kempis
>
> *Those who have given themselves up to God but imagine that they can go forward without a leader are surely deceiving themselves. The fugitives from Egypt had Moses, while those escaping from Sodom had an angel for a leader. . . . We must have someone very skilled, a doctor, for our septic wounds.* John Climacus
>
> *Wouldst thou walk in earnest towards devotion, seek some good man, who may guide and conduct thee; this is the best advice I can give thee.* Francis de Sales

When Augustine finally began his famous turn toward the Christian faith, he soon realized that he needed help. Great Christians are rarely produced in isolation; the most effective route to mature growth is working one-on-one with a mature Christian. Augustine wrote, "To Milan I came, to Ambrose the Bishop. . . . To him was I unknowingly led by Thee, that by him I might knowingly be led to Thee. That man of God received me as a father. . . . I hung on his words attentively."[1] Augustine's humility and wisdom in seeking spiritual direction helped to make him one of the most influential Christian bishops of all time.

It wasn't just at the beginning of his spiritual journey that Augustine sought counsel, however, and in this we can learn an even greater lesson. Later on in his life, Augustine wrote, "And Thou didst put into my mind, and it seemed good in my eyes, to go to Simplicianus [Ambrose's successor as bishop], who seemed to me a good servant of Thine; and Thy grace shone in him. I had heard also, that from his very youth he had lived most devoted unto Thee. Now he was grown into years; and by reason of so great age spent in such zealous following of Thy ways, he seemed to me likely to have learned much experience; and so he had. Out of which store, I wished that he would tell me which were the fittest way for one in my case to walk in Thy paths."[2]

Augustine was not a "self-made" Christian. Very few who go far are. We need spiritual coaching, which is something much different from the one sermon given to two hundred or more people every Sunday morning. The ancients urged Christians to find one-on-one relationships in which we can be challenged, corrected, and inspired to press on in the faith.

Why Do We Need a Spiritual Direction?

Why do we need help with spiritual direction? Four reasons may help explain the importance of this need.

[1]Augustine, *Confessions*, V:23.
[2]Ibid., VIII:1.

1. Because the Heart Is Deceitful

It shouldn't surprise us that the ancients, taking Scripture seriously (see Prov. 14:2), usually agreed on the need for wise, objective advice. One of the primary reasons for sharing our soul with another, wiser Christian, is that we lack the objectivity to see things accurately. As such, we are in a real danger of leading ourselves astray.

The unknown author of *The Cloud of Unknowing* writes, "as long as the soul dwells in this mortal body the accuracy of our understanding in perceiving spiritual things, most particularly God, is mingled with some manner of fantasy that tends to make our work unclean."[3]

Even the most mature Christian, according to John Climacus, hasn't outgrown the need for the input of others. Any one of us could be led astray. "A man, no matter how prudent, may easily go astray on a road if he has no guide."[4]

2. Because of Humility

More than mere prudence calls us to seek the counsel of others. Humility also moves us to get good advice. Thomas à Kempis wrote, "Who is so wise that he can fully know all things? Be not therefore too confident in thine own opinion; but be willing to hear the judgment of others."[5]

Notice that Thomas à Kempis said, "be willing to hear the judgment of others." We may not always agree with the input we receive, but humility demands we at least listen to the counsel of others. This is particularly true of those à Kempis calls "inexperienced."

[3]Anonymous, *The Cloud of Unknowing,* VIII:14.
[4]Climacus, *The Ladder of Divine Ascent,* 259.
[5]à Kempis, *The Imitation of Christ,* I:9:2.

"They that are yet but novices and inexperienced in the way of the Lord, unless they govern themselves by the counsel of discreet persons, may easily be deceived and broken to pieces. And if they will rather follow their own notions than trust to others who are more experienced, their end will be dangerous, at least if they are unwilling to be drawn away from their own fond conceit."[6]

We need direction to weed out those prejudices and attitudes that serve as roadblocks to further spiritual growth. A broken attitude can hold us down for years if we never realize its power over us, but a wise spiritual director might be able to spot such an attitude or faulty assumption within minutes. Why limit our growth to our own wisdom? Why not explore the fullness of life in Christ by learning from those who walk the journey with us?

3. Because We Have an Enemy

Another reason we need a spiritual friend is because we have a vicious and cunning spiritual enemy. The Bible says Satan is actively opposing us.[7] Hell is real. Hell wants us to sin. Hell plots to see our downfall. Plans are being made, right now, for you and me to fall. Since we have an enemy plotting our destruction, shouldn't we also have a friend who will plot our growth?

Our modern age has caused us to lose sight of spiritual realities the ancients took for granted. Ignatius understood hell's individual attention to the believer. He realized that Satan and his cohorts look at us as individuals, working to exploit our own personal weaknesses. Ignatius wrote, "The

[6]Ibid., III:7:2–3.
[7]See 1 Peter 5:8.

enemy observes very narrowly whether the soul be gross or delicate; and if it is delicate he strives to make it delicate to an extreme, that he may the more easily disturb and ruin it: . . . If he sees a soul consent to no sin . . . then the enemy, since he cannot cause it to fall into what has the appearance of sin, contrives to make it judge that there is sin where there is not, as in some word or insignificant thought. If the soul is gross, the enemy contrives to render it still more gross."[8]

Not only did Ignatius warn us that Satan pays us individual attention, but he also warned us that our perception of our spiritual growth can be rooted in error. Satan will manipulate our feelings; our own emotions will be used against us.

Because of such possibilities, we need an objective voice speaking truth into our souls. Ultimately, the Holy Spirit will be that voice, but the Spirit-inspired Scriptures encourage us to get many counselors. Bringing our concerns into the light is what Satan fears most, according to Ignatius of Loyola: "When the enemy of our human nature obtrudes on a just soul his wiles and deceits, he wishes and desires that they be furtively received and kept secret, but he is very displeased when they are discovered to a good confessor or some other spiritual person who knows his frauds and malice, because he infers that he cannot succeed in the wicked design he had conceived, as his evident frauds are laid open."[9]

If we really believe in hell, we must learn to live like we do, and protect ourselves against it. Satan has limits. He cannot overpower us, but he can deceive us. The best way to fight deception is to discuss our spiritual concerns with

[8]Ignatius Loyola, *Spiritual Exercises*, 119.
[9]Ibid., 110–11.

another believer who, being objective and acting within the gifting of the Holy Spirit, is less likely to be deceived. We should also seek someone who is aware of the mechanics of temptation and who has the ability to hear and be led by God. De Sales wrote:

"We should submit ourselves to the direction of a faithful friend, who, by the prudence and wisdom of his counsels, may guide us in all our actions, and secure us from the ambushes and deceits of the wicked one. Such a friend will be to us as a treasure of wisdom and consolation, in all our afflictions, our sorrows, and relapses; he will serve as a medicine to cure, and as a cordial to comfort our hearts in our spiritual disorders; he will guard us from evil, and make us advance in good; and should any infirmity befall us, he will assist in our recovery, and prevent its being unto death."[10]

4. Because Secrets Are Like Cancer

Yet another blessing of having a spiritual director is the death of secrets. Secrets are spiritual cancers. They allow a sinful action to become a habit until hell has a feast on what started out as "one little sin." Confession keeps us uncomfortable in our sin and forces us to seek a resolution.

Lying is the doorway to spiritual degeneration. Jesus called Himself the "truth" (John 14:6 NKJV) and Satan "a liar and the father of it" (John 8:44 NKJV). When we become mired in deceit we are following Satan, not Christ.

Scripture calls us to be people of the truth, and I've found that both truth and deceit are habits. A spiritual director moves us in the habit of truth. When we begin to live in the

[10]de Sales, *Introduction to a Devout Life*, 11.

light in front of one, it is easier to live in the light in front of all.

One of the church's main needs today is authenticity, especially in its leaders. Any type of ministry is intense; when you add secrets, particularly secrets of sin, ministry can become almost unbearable. Secrets allow Satan to blackmail us; rather than ministering in the freedom of Christ, we will forever be looking over our shoulder to cover that one little corner.

Just a couple of years ago, I couldn't have been as honest as I have been in sharing some of my own history and failings in this book, but I can't describe to you how freeing it is to slay the glittering image and finally have nothing to hide. The story of my life could be summed up like this: God has done some very good things in my life and I have done some very bad things, but through it all, God's grace has prevailed.

My willingness to be honest began when I was first honest with just one person. When I saw that person's love, and just as important, respect, remain constant, I was able to be more open with a slightly larger circle. At this point, we may very well be betrayed, but usually we will find walking in the light so freeing that we can simply pray for the one who betrayed us and ask God to grant that person His mercy. Soon we no longer want to be adored as much as we want to be real.

This call to authenticity doesn't mean I bare my entire soul with frivolity to anyone who cares to listen. Some things need to remain between us and only one or two other people, but very few things need to remain between us and God alone. Remember, the heart is deceitful, and secrecy provides a ripe atmosphere for sin to grow from an event, to a habit, to a character trait.

A healthy spiritual life is a life in which there are no secrets, no deceit, and no cover-up. Because God has provided for our forgiveness in Jesus Christ, there is no reason for a believer to suffer the pangs of conscience in isolation. Confession is God's gift to renew us and make us strong, not a duty.

I want to speak a special word particularly to those who have been victimized in any way. Be wary about letting a secret remain between you and your victimizer. An ongoing secret can be a form of ongoing abuse, for it gives the abuser power over you. The abuser may even derive a certain sadistic pleasure from the false "intimacy" of knowing something about you that nobody else knows. Prayerfully consider sharing your secret with a mature believer who loves you; you'll be amazed at the liberating power of truth and love.

Choosing a Spiritual Director

Because a spiritual director can play such an important role, we need to be very careful about the person we choose. Someone who has a problem with power or control, incorrect theology, or a lack of maturity can do more harm than good.

Thomas à Kempis urged that we seek someone who is "wise and conscientious" and "better" (or more mature) than ourselves.[11] In other words, it should be somebody we can look up to. Teresa of Avila urged that we find someone who can do what seems "impossible" to us; when we see the ease with which this person does the impossible, we will be encouraged and made "bold to fly." In this, little by little, we can imitate the parent. "Receiving this help is most beneficial; I know."[12]

[11]à Kempis, *The Imitation of Christ,* I:4:2.
[12]Teresa of Avila, *The Interior Castle,* III:2:12.

Teresa also urged that we seek after both wisdom and spiritual perception—though we may not necessarily find both of these in the same people. "It is good that at the beginning you speak about this vision under the seal of confession with a very learned man, for learned men will give us light. Or, with some very spiritual person, if there be one available; if there isn't, it's better to speak with a very learned man. Or with both a spiritual person and a learned man if both are at hand."[13]

It can be helpful to get two different perspectives—once, in one particularly intense circumstance, I sought four perspectives. I chose them according to what they could add to each other. Some people have a gift of wisdom; they understand how to apply general principles, but they are not very spiritually perceptive. Others may be spiritually perceptive but lack the background or understanding to put the perception to good use. Some people know the right answer but can't discern the problem. Others may not be skilled at discerning the problem but can provide some restorative counsel once the problem is known. If we find someone who is both wise and spiritually perceptive, we should be particularly thankful.

The director we choose should not be someone who will be threatened by our growth or who will imprison us within his or her own limitations. Teresa warned, "If the confessor is a person whom, although he practices prayer, the Lord has not led by this path, he will at once be frightened and condemn it. For this reason I advise you to have a confessor who is very learned and, if possible, also spiritual."[14]

[13]Ibid., VI:8:8.
[14]Ibid., VI:8:9.

I've found that a pastor, or any person for that matter, out to make a name for himself lacks the freedom to look objectively into another person's life without being threatened by it. He wants the person to participate in fulfilling his dreams, not necessarily the dreams God may have for the person.

The director should also be able to appreciate diversity. Spiritual disciplines, such as fasting, can be very helpful for some, but at other times they can be dangerous if they foster pride or are used as an attempt to gain God's favor. A director who treats every believer the same way is like a doctor who only prescribes one medicine regardless of the ailment. Such a director can actually poison one's faith.

"One man's medicine can be another man's poison, and something can be a medicine to the same man at one time and a poison at another. So I have seen an incompetent physician who by inflicting dishonor on a sick but contrite man produced despair in him, and I have seen a skillful physician who cut through an arrogant heart with the knife of dishonor and thereby drained it of all its foul-smelling pus."[15]

I was at a Christian retreat where two brothers were discussing marriage, and one of the men was really hurting. The other one immediately began talking to him about how he must be ignoring his wife, not building her up as she needed to be, taking her for granted, and so on. When I asked a few simple questions, however, it became immediately clear that this wasn't the case at all. An entirely different dynamic was at work. This brother needed healing and support, not condemnation. The one doing the counseling, we found, was

[15]Climacus, *The Ladder of Divine Ascent*, 233.

admittedly going through a period of conviction from God about his own sin toward his wife, and he was transferring it to this other brother.

People who are "full of themselves" can't direct others. A director must be as liberated as possible from his or her own experience in order to enter the experience of another. (And please understand, all of us can be full of ourselves at various points in our life. We all need to guard against this tendency.)

You may find, as I have, that when you first seek out someone to make a confession, he or she ends up confessing the same sin to you and then asking you for counsel! Press on and find another director, for such a person has not matured enough to care for someone else. I'm all for mutual sharing as long as both parties are getting the care they need. If the situation becomes one-sided, however, we need to find someone strong enough to help us in our weakness. (Incidentally, the possibility of receiving a confession is a good reason to live in holiness and full repentance. We don't want to be caught ashamed and unhealed if someone brings a confession to us and we have not addressed our own sin in that area.)

Another thing to look for in a director is an understanding of the devotional classics. Such an understanding frees the director from being a one-dimensional Christian who has only one answer. De Sales and Fénelon, for example, have much to teach us about temptation, but because they both lean toward quietism and mysticism, I'd have someone read John Owen's *Sin and Temptation* in between reading de Sales and Fénelon to give him or her a more systematic understanding of fighting sin and a more varied perspective.

John Climacus urged us to choose a spiritual director who is "old in wisdom rather than years,"[16] but I personally place a

[16]Ibid., 179.

high value on years as well. The young can be very spiritually perceptive, but wisdom takes time to develop.

Climacus also advised that we consider our own strengths and weaknesses and match those with the appropriate director. A director who does wonders for your friend may not serve you well at all.

"We should analyze the nature of our passions and of our obedience, so as to choose our director accordingly. If lust is your problem, do not pick for your trainer a worker of miracles who has a welcome and a meal for everyone. Choose instead an ascetic who will reject any of the consolation of food. If you are arrogant, let him be tough and unyielding, not gentle and accommodating. We should not be on the lookout for those gifted with foreknowledge and foresight, but rather for those who are truly humble and whose character and dwelling place match our weaknesses."[17]

Choosing a "soft" director is a particular temptation for those who have a problem with control. A high-powered pastor may purposefully choose a mushy "yes man" so he can feign accountability. A good director (or accountability group) should not be easily manipulated or intimidated by us.

Climacus urged us to thoroughly check out our spiritual director but once we've made our choice to respect his or her role.

When humbly and with true longing for salvation we resolve to bend the neck and entrust ourselves to another in the Lord, there is something to be done before we start. If there happens to be any cunning in us, any prudence, then we should question, examine, and . . . put to the test our master, so that there is no mistaking the sailor for the helmsman, the patient for the doctor,

[17]Ibid., 119.

the passionate for the dispassionate man, the sea for the harbor—with the resulting shipwreck of our soul. But having once entered the stadium of holy living and obedience, we can no longer start criticizing the umpire, even if we should notice some faults in him. After all, he is human and if we start making judgments, then our submissiveness earns no profit.

If we wish to preserve unshaken faith in our superiors, we must write their good deeds indelibly in our hearts and preserve them in our memories so that, when the demons scatter distrust of them among us, we can repel them by what we have retained in our minds. . . . When the thought strikes you to judge or condemn your superior, leap away as though from fornication."[18]

One of Satan's favorite ploys to keep us from truth is to make us despise the messenger of truth. If our director speaks a difficult word to us, we will be tempted to ignore the truth by trying to find the same or a similar fault in our director. This is nothing but evasion. Just because somebody else has the same fault, even if that somebody is our director, doesn't mean we don't need to work on it.

With such a demanding role to play, it is clear that a spiritual director should not be chosen casually. Francis de Sales wrote, " 'For this end, choose one amongst a thousand,' says Avila; but I say, choose one amongst ten thousand; for there are fewer than can be imagined who are capable of this office. He must be a man of charity, learning, and prudence. If any one of these three qualities be wanting in him, there is danger."[19]

How, then, can we find one if they are so rare? Francis de Sales urged that we make it a matter of earnest prayer. "Be-

[18]Ibid., 92–93.
[19]de Sales, *Introduction to a Devout Life,* 13.

seech God, with the greatest importunity, to furnish you with one who may be according to his own heart; and be assured that he will rather send you an angel from heaven, as he did to young Tobias, than fail to grant your request."[20]

Sharing Sin

There is a proper process for sharing our sins and temptations once we've found an able director. First, we must be determined to be absolutely honest. It is no good choosing a confessor and then being half-hearted about it. While we don't need a confessor to be forgiven, a confessor can play an important part in our spiritual health, but only if we're open and honest.

Francis de Sales urged the believer to tell a spiritual director "how long a time you have continued in your sin; for the length of time is an aggravation of the evil." He continued, "We must . . . tell the fact, the motive, and the continuance of our sins. For though we are not bound to declare venial [*venial* means a slight offense, or a grave offense committed without reflection] sins, nor absolutely obliged to confess them, yet those who desire to cleanse their souls perfectly and attain to holy devotion, must be careful to make their spiritual physician acquainted with the evil of which they desired to be cured, no matter how small it may be."[21]

Think of sin as a disease that is slowly destroying your health. You would tell a physician about every symptom, every nuance, every complication, to give him or her as accurate a description as possible. Have the same attitude toward sin.

[20]Ibid., 12.
[21]Ibid., 107–8.

It is different in nature than a disease, but if anything, it is even more deadly, for it has spiritual as well as physical complications. Don't give sin any place to hide. If nothing else, this is an excellent exercise in humility.

The second way we must confess is face-to-face. Confession forces us to face the reality of our sin. Why is it that confession with God can seem so easy but confessing to a brother or sister in Christ seems so hard? It is because our grasp of the presence and power of God is so pitifully small. We aren't really confessing to God; we're confessing to ourselves. When we confess to another believer, face-to-face, we sense Christ's presence in that person—and then we see the true nature of our sins. This helps to break the hold of repeated sins. John Climacus wrote, "Confession is like a bridle that keeps the soul which reflects on it from committing sin, but anything left unconfessed we continue to do without fear as if in the dark."[22]

In this sense confession is a spotlight, forcing us to look at our sins in the full light of God's truth, not letting us pretend it is merely a slight indiscretion. We need to face the one to whom we're confessing, look him or her in the eyes, and be humiliated as we state our sins and admit our wrongdoing. We need to let the intensity of the moment burn the sin out of us!

We need to be honest about our temptations as well as our sins. It is not God's will that we suffer in silence, alone and isolated, carrying out an unseen battle with Satan. When we are tempted, we need encouragement, perspective, and instruction.

De Sales exhorted, "The sovereign remedy against all

[22]Climacus, *The Ladder of Divine Ascent*, 107.

temptations, whether great or small, is to lay open your heart, and communicate its suggestions, feelings, and affections to your director; for you must observe, that the first condition that the enemy of salvation makes with a soul which he desires to seduce is to keep silence. . . . Whereas God, on the other hand, by his inspirations, requires that we should make them known to our superiors and directors."[23]

The church has plenty of servants who are skilled at talking to large crowds, but there is a virtual famine of Christians who can perform "soul surgery," dealing with confused and struggling Christians one on one as their spiritual director.

The Call to Be a Spiritual Director

Where are the brave souls who will plunge into this private work of a spiritual director? The first chapter of this book talked about spiritual goals. Becoming a skilled spiritual director is a very laudable goal. It will mean we have to be ruthless with our own failings and honest with others about our own faults; it will mean we need to draw ever closer to Christ. I have found, however, that the only thing more fulfilling than rapturous prayer is releasing someone else to enjoy that same prayer. The only thing more thrilling than being healed, gradually or suddenly, from a troublesome sin or trait is to help another be healed of a sin or character weakness.

Francis de Sales, that great bishop who took the time to minister to individuals—who, indeed, despite his fame was willing to preach to "crowds" numbering less than half a dozen—wrote, "It is painful, I confess, to direct souls in particular; but it is a pain that gives a comfort like that which

[23]de Sales, *Introduction to a Devout Life*, 300.

is felt by the laborers in the harvest and vintage, who are never better pleased than when they have most to do, and when their burdens are the heaviest. It is a labor which refreshes and revives the heart by the sweet delight it excites in those who are engaged in it."[24]

Just recently, I spent sixty minutes one evening on the phone with a brother who was struggling. Some years ago the call would have felt like an intrusion—that's how self-centered I was as I guarded my "recreation" time in front of the television. But since God has been freeing me in an ongoing process for several years, I've found that real ministry is far more refreshing than mindless entertainment. Our souls seek relationships, not images.

Will we leave the crowds and minister to the one? Are our lives even in shape to do it? This is a high calling and an exciting work for those who will listen to God's direction.

Reflections

Are you keeping any secrets that are hindering your spiritual life? Consider whether sharing these with a trustworthy individual might not bring health and healing.

Spend a few minutes in prayer and write down the names of those who you feel might be able to give you appropriate direction. Spend the next week or so asking God to confirm one or more of these people who might be able to give you formal or informal counsel.

Are you in a spiritual condition to counsel others? Have you repented of your sins and are you growing in grace and character? Read over some of the qualifications of a good spiritual director. Are you being called to become one?

[24]Ibid., author's preface, xix.

Afterword

> *Who is he who will devote himself to be close to me?*
> Jeremiah 30:21 (NIV)

Near Walden Pond, just outside of Boston, you can see what remains of the foundation that held the cabin of Henry David Thoreau. Next to the foundation site is a pile of rocks, by now a fairly large one. Out of respect for Thoreau's life and writings, visitors have taken their turn adding one stone to the pile. There is no sign anywhere telling people to do this. If you just walked by, you might wonder, "What's that pile of stones for?"

In some ways I felt that writing a book would be like adding a stone to that pile. What's the use? There are already so many; can one more make any difference? But I went ahead and wrote the book, just as I added a stone to the pile. Here's why.

Thoreau was a nature mystic who uncovered a portion of truth, but became so enamored with the beauty of what God had made that he missed the God behind it. I share Thoreau's respect for the outdoors; his prescription that everyone should spend several hours outside every day could only do us good. Indeed, it's when I'm outside, surrounded by what God has made, that I feel truly alive.

I feel alive, though, because the God who made it surrounds me, and that's the difference. Thoreau comes close, but he kept his eyes too low. So why pay him any respect? Like few of us, he uncovered an important truth. Like many of us, however, he let a smaller truth eclipse the larger truth.

Thoreau's relinquishing the eternal for the created is not unlike the parents who become so enamored with the beauty and life of their child, or their desire for the child that God seems to be withholding, that they begin worshiping the created instead of the Creator. It is not unlike the pastor who becomes so fulfilled by serving God that he begins worshiping his church rather than the God who makes the church. We can still learn from these people, but they have allowed the temporal to eclipse the eternal.

This world is full of good quests that begin to pull us away from our first love because we live with a bent heart. Christian bookstores carry good books and helpful books, and I've read many of them. We need to know how to handle our finances, be committed to our families, stand up for righteousness in politics, and build our churches. But these quests will do nothing but sap our strength if our roots are not sunk deep into an intimate walk with our heavenly Father. Why wash the windshield of a car that won't run? Why water a seed that's never been planted?

The purpose of this book is really to cry out the words given to us by God through Jeremiah: "Who is he who will devote himself to be close to me?" (Jer. 30:21 NIV). Is a close, continuing walk with God really the desire of our hearts? Do we long, more than anything else, to know Him and be known by Him?

The struggle of the Christian life is really a struggle to maintain the centrality of God in our day-to-day lives. The peripheral matters are always pushing in, trying to steal our hearts away. That's why, if we're not consciously seeking the face of God, striving to know Him, we're likely falling away. We're told that King Rehoboam did evil because "he did not prepare his heart to seek the LORD" (2 Chron. 12:14 NKJV).

As I mentioned earlier in this book, what we really need, what the world is really waiting to see, is a group of people dedicated to living the Christian life. This is the true calling of a mail carrier, a university professor, a pastor, or a homemaker. We need to discuss various theological points, but even more precious in God's sight is whether we are living them instead of arguing about them.[1]

If the wisdom of the ancients has awakened any heart toward this end and moved that heart a little further along the way, then the analogy of writing this book is not like adding a stone to that pile of rocks. It is like picking up the stone from the pile, walking down the hill to Walden Pond, and dropping the stone in the middle. The rock will soon be swallowed and forgotten, as this book will eventually be, but the ripples it created as it touched the surface will continue for a little longer, perhaps until somebody else comes along and drops another rock.

The ripples might be hidden; they may be seen only in a locked room as a believer pours out his or her heart to God in a new and fresh way, or in a silent forest as a man renews his vows of love and commitment to his Creator, or in an empty church, as a pastor or church member returns to his or her first love. But I am confident that God wants to drop the rock. I believe He wants to call us back. I'm certain He

---

[1]One of my most humorous memories of seminary is seeing two students almost get into a fistfight over the meaning of the Greek word *phileo*, which means, of course, "brotherly love"!

is reaching out for those who will devote themselves to be close to Him. And I have great confidence in God's ability to make ripples effective—even more effective than the dropped rock that caused them.

I placed the stone on the pile. It will be up to you, the reader, to see whether it gets moved to the pond, creating the ripples. You hold the rock in your hand now.

For information about the Center for Evangelical Spirituality, write:
        Center for Evangelical Spirituality
        P.O. Box 1596
        Manassas, Virginia 22110

Appendix

Selected Bibliography of Christian Spiritual Classics

This list is by no means exhaustive, and, in fact, is rather limited, but it should serve as an introduction to many of the classics mentioned in this work.

Saint Augustine, *The Confessions of Saint Augustine* (c. 400)

Long considered the classic of all time, many modern readers will find this book difficult reading with scattered wisdom. The genre itself will seem unfamiliar and slightly wordy to many evangelicals.

John Climacus, *The Ladder of Divine Ascent* (c. 640)

The classic of eastern Christendom, written to monks, this book calls for a high commitment and the message may seem harsh, but the book is worthy of the attention it has received.

Anonymous, *The Cloud of Unknowing* (late fourteenth century)

This book is very mystical, but with real gems sprinkled throughout. Evangelicals might find the full "program" of little interest or benefit, but those who take the time to read it will find considerable wisdom.

Thomas à Kempis, *The Imitation of Christ* (c. 1418)
This is probably one of the most popular spiritual classics. À Kempis focused on rigorous spiritual training as a necessary part of Christian living. His work is a good counter to "soft" Christianity.

Ignatius Loyola, *The Spiritual Exercises of Saint Ignatius Loyola* (1548)
Full of very practical advice for monks, this book also offers many helpful insights for evangelicals.

John of the Cross, *Ascent of Mount Carmel* and *Dark Night of the Soul* (c. 1587)
Author of these two mystical classics, John was recognized as a highly gifted spiritual director (he was Teresa of Avila's director for three years). In these works he provides many helpful insights into the spiritual life, especially the stages that Christians go through. One of my favorite writers, John of the Cross wrote with an unparalleled passion for God.

Teresa of Avila, *Interior Castle* (1588)
This is a relatively short book on prayer, emphasizing spiritual visions leading to spiritual betrothal and marriage.

Francis de Sales, *Introduction to a Devout Life* (1609)
This is a unique spiritual book in that Francis wrote for laypeople, not a religious community. His desire was to see the ordinary tradesman learn to grow spiritually, recognizing that they needed different advice than members of a religious community. This book is very practical with several helpful meditations.

John Owen, *Sin and Temptation* (1656–1667)
This is actually a compilation of three of John Owen's treatises that have now been collected by Dr. James Houston. Owen's teaching on sin and temptation is must reading for every Christian. At the

time of this writing, the book is out of print, but you can locate the three treatises—*Of the Mortification of Sin in Believers, Of Temptation,* and *The Nature, Power and Deceit of Indwelling Sin,* in a collection of John Owen's works.

Blaise Pascal, *Pensées* (1670)

Pascal was a brilliant man in both science and devotion; the *Pensées* comprise an unfinished collection of his random thoughts. It's haphazard reading, but there are some real gems for those who wade through the collection.

Brother Lawrence, *The Practice of the Presence of God* (1692)

Brother Lawrence was a very humble man with an extraordinary sense of living in God's presence. This little book includes several letters and conversations Brother Lawrence had with others who wanted to learn from his experience.

Francois Fénelon, *Christian Perfection* (1704–1717)

Along with John of the Cross, Fénelon is one of my favorites. Fénelon wrote as a wealthy mystic living in the upper strata of French society. The temptations faced by the elite several hundred years ago are remarkably similar to those faced by middle-class evangelicals today. This is one of the most helpful spiritual classics I've read; it's one you may want to read over and over.

William Law, *A Serious Call to a Devout and Holy Life* (1728)

This is a rigorous treatise written by a devout Puritan. It is very helpful and challenging but could be dangerous for a person who isn't rooted in grace because it might lead some into an unhealthy legalism.

Jonathan Edwards, *A Treatise Concerning Religious Affections* (1746)
Discusses those who are "truly pious" by examining and discussing various religious affections.

Credits

The following publishers have generously given permission to use extended quotations from copyrighted works. From The Cloud of Unknowing, *translated by Ira Progoff.* © *1957 by Ira Progoff. Used by permission of Bantam, Doubleday, Dell Publishing Group. From* William Law: A Serious Call to a Devout and Holy Life, *edited by Paul Stanwood.* © *1978 by The Missionary Society of St. Paul the Apostle in the State of New York. Used by permission of Paulist Press. From* John Climacus: The Ladder of Divine Ascent, *translated by Colm Luibheid and Norman Russell.* © *1982 by The Missionary Society of St. Paul the Apostle in the State of New York. Used by permission of Paulist Press. From* Teresa of Avila: The Interior Castle, *trans. by Kieran Kavanaugh, O.C.D. and Otilio Rodriguez, O.C.D.* © *1979 by the Washington Province of Discalced Carmelites, Inc. Used by permission of Paulist Press. From* John of the Cross: Selected Writings, *edited by Kieran Kavanaugh, O.C.D.* © *1987 by the Washington Province of the Discalced Carmelites, Inc. Used by permission of Paulist Press. From* The Practice of the Presence of God *by Brother Lawrence. Used by permission of Forward Movement Publications. From* Christian Perfection *by Fénelon.* © *1947 by Harper and Row. Used by permission of Bethany House Publishers. From* The Imitation of Christ *by Thomas à Kempis.* © *1984, Moody Bible Institute of Chicago. Moody Press. Used by permission. From* Pensées *by Blaise Pascal.* © *1966 by A. J. Krailsheimer. Used by permission of Penguin Books Ltd. (London). From* Sin and Temptation *by John Owen, edited by Dr. James M. Houston.* © *1983 by James M. Houston. Used by permission of Dr. James M. Houston.*